Our Salvation: Beauty for Ashes

Jeremy Kropf

ACKNOWLEDGMENTS

A very heartfelt thank you to all my friends and family who helped me in writing this book. It was a lengthy process and I would never have finished it without their support. In particular, thank you to Daniel J. Caram, without whose prompting I would never have even embarked on this journey. He encouraged me through it and gave valuable input. Thank you to Cameron Walcott for sharing his thoughts and assisting me in publishing the book. Also, thanks to my mom for her editing and fixing my many mistakes. Thank you to Eric Warner for the beautiful cover design. It is an absolutely stunning piece of work and I am truly grateful. Most of all, thank you to our Lord and Savior Jesus Christ, in whom we live and move and have our being, and through whom, we are saved.

CONTENTS

Introduction 1

Free will – Do We Have It? 3

God's Sovereignty 13

Mixing Sovereignty with Free Will 23

God Determines and Man Chooses 35

Election 45

Sin Nature 59

Grace 65

Repentance 75

The Walk of Faith 85

Assurance 99

Epilogue 115

INTRODUCTION

What is salvation? It is the great and wonderful truth that God, through the death and resurrection of Christ, has reconciled us to Himself, adopted us as His children and someday will welcome us into a glorious, eternal home with Him. Most Christians would agree with this statement. It is indeed our glorious hope. However, the more you look at the process of how God does this, the more diverging opinions you find.

For instance, who is saved? Is it everyone? Are there conditions for being saved? If there are conditions, why do some meet those conditions and others do not? Is it because some people choose to be saved while others do not? Or maybe, it is God who chooses, and people do not have any choice in the matter? Those are just a few questions and there could be a lot more.

I do believe that the Bible has a lot to say on this subject, and can give us a lot of guidance in this area. We are going to approach this topic by taking every scripture at face value. While it might not be possible to narrow everything down to a precise answer, I do believe that Scripture gives us what I would call "guideposts." By this, I mean that Scripture sets down certain parameters and the truth has to be within them. This concept will be particularly important as we move forward in this study.

A simplistic example of how we could understand these "guideposts" is in the game "Twenty Questions". This is a simple game where one person thinks of an object and one or more other people try to figure out what that object is by asking no more than twenty questions. The rules also dictate that these questions need to be asked in such a way that they can be answered with a simple "yes" or "no". By asking the right questions, you narrow down the possibilities until you have deduced the only thing that remains.

In a similar way, I believe that Scripture narrows down a lot of possibilities for us. It does show us some things that are absolutely true and others that are absolutely untrue. Now, when we come to matters of our salvation, I believe this is a faithful way to examine Scripture. A passage should mean what it appears to mean. It should not have to be twisted to have a meaning that we would prefer. Rather, if it appears to present a conflict with another passage, could it not rather be just a guidepost on the other side? For instance, one passage may be defining the western boundary, while another defines the eastern boundary. The truth of how God deals with us lies in between those two guideposts.

I believe this is very important, because one of the greatest difficulties for those who take the Bible seriously is what to do with passages that appear to not conform to what we believe. Oftentimes, we have the tendency to focus upon the verses that we like, while others who believe differently focus on the particular verses that they like. We take a particular passage, elevate it to authoritative status above all others and then, from that point of view, make the rest of Scripture conform. This happens on all sides of an issue. In this study, I will endeavor to give all Scriptures equal weight, and not to shy away from those passages that do not line up as easily with my point of view.

FREE WILL –
DO WE HAVE IT?

Do we have free will? Are we actually making choices or do we just "think" we are? This is something that has been considered in many different cultures in one form or another over the past few millennia. It is common for people to talk of its being "fate" that you meet your future spouse. If someone seems to get away with a wrong action for a time, but then something unexpected happens to them, some will use the more Eastern word, Karma. Beliefs of this kind are very widespread. We see an example of such a belief in Acts 28:3-6. There we find that when pagans saw that the Apostle Paul had been bitten by a snake, they assumed that he must have been a murderer. They presumed that although he had escaped the shipwreck alive, "justice" had finally caught up with him. Popular movies like Star Wars use phrases such as "It is your destiny!"

These all imply a belief that, at least to some extent, events are predetermined. The details, of course, vary wildly, but the core concept of some kind of deterministic belief remains. Modern science also has some difficulties here. If we are only physical creatures that simply respond to inputs and produce corresponding outputs, then free choice is nothing more than an illusion. This would be the logical conclusion if we were no more than simply matter – consisting solely of a physical brain and a physical body.

If we did not have free will, a difficult question arises: "How do we deal with people who do things that we would consider wrong?" If they did not have free will, then their choices were predetermined, and they literally could not have chosen to do otherwise. They were forced to make that wrong choice. If they were forced to make that wrong choice, then how can we punish them? But, it goes much further than that. If we ourselves, when evaluating someone who does not have free will, do not have free will either, then we have no choice but to respond in the way that we are predisposed to respond.

If all this were true, those who chose to do certain things had no *real* choice in the matter. The choice in that case would only be an illusion. Also, anything that we do in the future will not really be a choice. When we hear someone say something, we will either respond and believe their argument or reject it, not because we actively choose it, but simply because it is our response to the input we have received up to the present moment.

The implications of this are enormous. To follow such a line of thought is quite startling. It destroys the very foundation of ethics and values. It implies that those who were engaged in evils, such as slavery, could not have chosen otherwise, and also, that we could not choose otherwise but to now think of those things as ethically repugnant. Ethics would then cease to have any true moral basis, but would rather be turned into the average of the collective group-think that is only valid at a specific point in time. Truth itself ceases to have any real meaning, as it can never have any hope of actually being discovered. Instead, it would be more appropriate to describe things as being inevitable. They either happen or do not – the moral compass has no basis.

The preceding thought experiment shows the logical conclusion of full determinism—where every choice is predetermined. This would be a world without any free will. But is this the world we are living in? Are all our actions fully determined? Do we have free will?

All our intuition tells us that we do indeed have choices. In fact, we deliberate many times on many things. While some might say this is an exercise in futility, this does not seem to be the most logical explanation. We sometimes wrestle over decisions precisely because those decisions and choices are indeed real. Some of the decisions are trivial, while some are extremely important.

When I was a boy, sometimes I would go with my mother to the grocery store. While there, I would be able to buy some candy. I had a limited amount of money to spend, and I had to choose what I thought was best. There was a certain candy bar that I liked the most; however, it was just one candy bar, and would be eaten in less than five minutes. Certainly, I would really enjoy eating that candy bar, but in a few short moments, it would all be gone. Now, for about the same price I could also get a box of mints. These did not taste nearly as good as the candy bar, although I also really enjoyed them. The difference was that this box of mints would last so much longer than the candy bar. So, I had a choice to make – was I going to choose the better tasting candy bar, or the longer lasting mints? I could easily spend 15 minutes trying to decide, while my mother was shopping for the other things that were needed for the household!

I believe it is an example of what we all have done on occasion. There are certainly much bigger things in life than choosing what candy we are going to eat. There are the crucial decisions: what job to take, whom to marry, what church to attend, and of course, most of all, the decision to follow Christ (if indeed you assent that it "is" a decision). We have all experienced this decision process. Intuitively, we feel as if we are making real decisions, but what does Scripture have to say?

Scripture tells us that we have a free will. Later we will look at what the Bible has to say about God's control of things, but first, we are laying down the guidepost that we have a free will. Let's call it the "Western boundary." Why do we say that Scripture says that we have a free will?

First, because there are so many passages that advise us to make right choices. What is the point of scriptures exhorting us to choose rightly, if the choices are not in fact real? The passages are so numerous that it would hardly be practical to list them all, so I will list just a few examples.

There is the example of Adam and Eve in the Garden of Eden (Gen. 3). God specifically told them not to eat of the tree of the knowledge of good and evil. Eve was tempted by the serpent and chose to sin. Eve gave the fruit to Adam, and he too chose to eat and thereby sin entered the world (Rom. 5:12). Adam and Eve chose to disobey God's command. They ate the forbidden fruit and sin came into the human race. It came through a choice to disobey the command of God. Every passage of scripture that refers to this incident attributes the fall to the choices of Adam and Eve. There are not many people that would contend with this statement.

Let us look next at a very well-known Scripture passage: Joshua 24:14-28. Here, Joshua exhorts the people to choose whom they will serve. He then declares, *"As for me and my house, we will serve the LORD."* We can say that the people were not actually making a choice, but that God had already predetermined what they would do and they had no true alternative in the matter. However, that does not appear to line up with the text. The entire text concerns the people making a choice to serve the Lord.

Deuteronomy 30:19-20, which occurs a number of years earlier than Joshua 24, essentially expresses the same thoughts as Joshua 24. In it, Moses commands the children of Israel to make a choice —— to serve the Lord and receive life, or instead to choose death. The choice was put before them and they were expected to make a decision. Obviously, it was not just for that moment, but the implication was that they would have to continually choose life, to continually serve the Lord, so that they would continually receive the blessings.

The call of God for people to turn from their evil ways to be restored is throughout all of Scripture (e.g. Pro. 1:23; Is. 55:6-7; Jer. 3:22; Jer. 31:18-20; Ez. 14:6; Hos. 14:1; Acts 3:19, 26:20). Throughout the books of the prophets, the Lord is pleading with His people to turn from their wicked ways so that they do not die. Ezekiel 18:30-32 is one such example. In it, the Lord urges His people to repent and states that He has no pleasure in the death of anyone. This kind of a statement only makes sense if the people could actually make the choice to repent.

Ezekiel 33:11 carries a similar theme. Here again, the Lord pleads with His people to turn from their evil ways back to Him. He assures them that He has no pleasure in the death of the wicked and says, *"Why will you die, O house of Israel?"* Again, we see the heart of God pleading with His people.

It is apparent from these passages that God is trying to reason with His people and declaring that He does not have any pleasure in their judgment. He is asking them to repent and is marveling that they are continuing on this path of destruction.

This presents an issue. God states clearly that He has no pleasure in the death of the wicked, and yet it is happening. They are coming under judgment. He pleads with them to change, and yet if they do not have free will, then they have no ability to change. Instead, you would have to assume that God is pleading for them to do the impossible and asking the question, "Why will you die, O house of Israel?" in more of a mocking tone than anything else. The text certainly does not lead us to this conclusion. Instead, it clearly supports that man has free will, that God calls man to repentance.

The New Testament echoes this theme in 2 Peter 3:9, where we are told that the Lord is not willing that any should perish, but that all should come to repentance. God does not want anyone to perish, and yet some do. Here is an apparent problem. We believe in an omnipotent God who wants something to happen. He wants everyone to come to repentance, and yet we know that not everyone does. This leaves us with the fact that God wants something to happen, and yet it does not. There must be something else that is also happening.

If you concede that God also wants to allow His creatures to have free will, then you have a workable solution. If you exclude the possibility of free will, you have to acknowledge that God, for whatever reason, desired to punish some of His creatures and even though He says He desires all to be saved, He really only ever intended to save some of them. Only one of these answers really seems to satisfy the text of 2 Peter 3:9, and that is the fact that we have a free will that God has chosen not to violate to the extent of forcing a person to repent and believe. Now, this free will is in no way without restraint – there are many restraints placed upon it, but again, this will be saved for another section. We are just establishing the "Western boundary" at this point.

John 3:16 is often cited as proof that "whoever believes" will not perish, but will have everlasting life. Some will counter this by simply saying that it is not possible to believe on your own, but rather that you only believe if God has selected you to believe. Thus they hold that there is no human choice involved in that belief, but that rather it is simply that God has given them that faith. They will usually point to verses such as Ephesians 2:8 to support this.

Ephesians 2:8 states, *"For by grace you have been saved through faith. And this is not your own doing; it is the gift of God…"* The question is, what is the gift of God – is it faith, or is it salvation? Many Biblical scholars, with much better knowledge of the Greek than I, have done extensive work on this verse. Some will say one way, and some another. Therefore, if you read one English translation, it may lean one way and another translation will lend itself to the other interpretation. If nothing else, this tells me that we should not insist upon a particular interpretation of a verse that could be read either way. Therefore, while this verse could support either reading, it should not serve as a foundation verse for establishing a doctrine that then is used to interpret other scriptures.

Regardless, what is certainly clear from this verse (and other passages) is that we are not saved because of our own merit. We are not saved because we are good people. We are saved by the grace of God. It is a free gift. None of us have earned it. Although all of this will be covered later, this is a fundamental Christian belief that should always be clearly emphasized.

Returning to the thought of the free will of man, we come to Luke 13:34. It states, *"O Jerusalem, Jerusalem, the city that kills the prophets and stones those who are sent to it! How often would I have gathered your children together as a hen gathers her brood under her wings, and you were not willing!"* (ESV). Here, Jesus says of Jerusalem that many times He had longed to gather her children under His wings, but they were not willing. We see God's desire to cover and protect Jerusalem, but they chose otherwise. God wanted something, but they wanted something different, and they, not God, got what they wanted. God allowed their free-will choice, even when His desire was different!

There is a line of reasoning that goes like this. "Ever since the fall of Adam, man has become wholly sinful. As such, he is unable to believe God. It is not possible for him to have faith. He cannot repent. The only way he can do this is if God first regenerates his heart and irresistibly causes him to believe. If God gives a man grace, he will always believe. If God chooses not to give the grace, then a man can never believe. Faith is a gift of God that He gives, according to His own sovereign choice, to whom He will. Those who receive the faith do so through the irresistible grace of the Holy Spirit, and those who do not receive the faith do not receive it because God did not give it to them."

Those who espouse such a view do so to make it clear that salvation is all of God, not of man, lest anyone should boast. I wholeheartedly agree that salvation is all of God, and not of man, but the specifics that I believe Scripture supports are quite different. That line of reasoning is flawed in that it does not allow any place for the free will of man. Now, none of this means that the free will is unrestrained. However, it is very difficult to imagine that God gave us so many passages in His Word where He pleads with His people to make a choice, if they actually had no ability to choose. Those passages are throughout the law, the prophets and the New Testament.

If the above point-of-view were indeed true and people had no choice, Luke 13:34 would have Jesus saying something like this: "O Jerusalem, Jerusalem, the city that kills the prophets and stones those who are sent to it! How often would I have gathered your children together as a hen gathers her brood under her wings, but **I did not really want to give you the grace to repent and so** you were not willing!" Note the bold writing. Obviously, this is a gross distortion of the text! But if you believe that the only way that a person repents is if God gives them irresistible grace, then that is really what Jesus was saying. However, the text simply does not support this interpretation.

It is true that if you took a single text in isolation, you could easily distort it to emphasize one truth or another. Also, not every verse should be expected to give a fully balanced view on every subject. The problem is that these are not isolated texts. The Word of God is full of examples such as this. In Nehemiah 9:30, we read: *"Many years you bore with them and warned them by your Spirit through your prophets. Yet they would not give ear. Therefore you gave them into the hand of the peoples of the lands"* (ESV). Again, we see the same thought – God, through His Spirit warned the people, called out to them; yet they would not listen. Therefore, they suffered the consequences. Scripture is consistent on this.

We have free will. We can make choices: simple everyday life decisions and also moral ones. While we are certainly limited by our nature and our circumstances, the choices are, nevertheless, real. God pleads with us to make right choices. He pleads with us to humble ourselves and repent, for it is the humble who receive the grace of God (Jam. 4:6-10, 1 Pet. 5:6). However, for the proud, who are wise in their own eyes and strong in themselves, there is very little hope (Pr. 26:12).

Before we move on from this section of free will and choice, there is one more thing that I want to consider. There are two things that we are specifically told in Scripture that Jesus marveled at: a person's faith (Mt. 8:10), and people's unbelief (Mk. 6:6). If there is no human choice involved in these things, then how can it be that Jesus can marvel at them? If it is as simple as God gave faith to some and not to others, then why would the Gospels portray Jesus as wondering at either their great faith or lack thereof? Also, would you not expect there to be many verses in the gospels and the prophets that, instead of making it look like God is marveling that people are not repenting, state that God never chose them and so they will not be receiving any faith? To be sure, there are verses that emphasize the role that God plays in conviction, in drawing and in bringing a person to repentance (e.g. Jn. 6:44, 16:7-14), but these verses cannot override all the other scriptures. Scripture asserts both man's free will and God's sovereignty. Therefore, both must be true.

We have just set the first guidepost in the ground: man has free will. Whatever else we see as we continue our exploration, we cannot be faithful to Scripture and remove this guidepost. It must stand.

GOD'S SOVEREIGNTY

What do we mean when we say that God is sovereign? We simply mean that God is in charge. He is ruling over everything. He has rights over all creation – if for no other reason than that He made it all. He made not only all the material things, the atoms, the photons, the ions, the electrons, etc., but He also made all the laws that govern our entire physical universe. Not coincidentally, He also made the moral laws by which He has chosen to govern all things.

I make this last point, because God, if He wanted to, could rule as a complete despot. Since He made us and everything else, He could do just as He wishes. Instead, we see a God who is full of love and mercy humbling himself, taking on the form of a servant and suffering a cruel death that was only given to the most despicable of people (cf. Php. 2:5-8). He was mocked and tortured by His own creation. If there exists a greater injustice in the universe, I cannot think of it. Yet He chose it willingly, to show us His mercy and power. He may be entitled to be arbitrary and rule harshly, but that is not how our God is.

However, make no mistake, God is in control. This world is not spinning out of His hand while He is trying to keep it all together. God is not surprised by anything that happens. Daniel 4 gives us a poignant example of when God decided to show us that He rules in the affairs of men. Nebuchadnezzar learned that lesson in a very painful way. Three times in that chapter it says that the Most High rules in the kingdom of men and gives it to whom he desires. God decides who is raised up and who is not (Ps. 75:6-7). He sets up presidents, the good and the bad. He is in control.

If man has free-will (and we just saw in the previous chapter that the Bible shows that he does), then how is God still in control? In many ways, this relates to God's foreknowledge, although by foreknowledge we do not simply mean God knowing what will happen beforehand. While it is true that God knows what is going to happen before it does, God's existence is not limited to time like ours is. In a certain sense, He is outside of time. He sees tomorrow as clearly as He sees yesterday. He knows all things: the eternal past and the eternal future.

God does not dwell in time, because He created time and thus has to reside outside of it. This has been believed by Christians since the earliest stages of Christianity. The early church father Ignatius wrote that the Father and Son were before the beginning of time.[1] St. Augustine wrote that the world and God were not in the same time continuum. Rather, God is completely outside of time. Interestingly enough, Einstein's theory of relativity would lead to the same conclusion – if something is outside of material space, it must then of necessity also be outside of time. This belief about God has been held by much of the Christian community for close to 2,000 years.

God sees the future, not just in the sense that He knows what will happen, but in the sense that He is already there. He is ever-present. Some posit that because God **knows** everything that will happen, or is omniscient, that He must therefore **cause** everything to happen. They suppose that these two things are fully intertwined. The basis for this would be that if God creates things and puts them in motion then the cause and effect means that everything must be caused by God – the ultimate causer. However, this does not necessarily need to be the case. It would have to be the case if we were purely material beings, because the laws of nature would dictate that we would have to respond according to the dictates of the original creation. However, we are not just material beings – we are conscious beings with a free will, as we examined before.

When we consider God's foreknowledge, He does not just know everything that will **actually** happen, He also knows all the **contingencies**. He knows what would happen, what people **would** choose to do, when presented with certain choices. This carries with it a lot of implications, which we shall examine in due course. The Bible shows this in at least two places, which we will briefly examine.[2]

In 1 Samuel 23, we read the story of David and the city of Keilah. While David was running for his life from King Saul, he and his men delivered the people of the city from the Philistines. After that, Saul heard that David was still there, and prepared to go down to the city. David then asked the Lord some important questions. First, he asked if Saul would come down to Keilah. The Lord answered in the affirmative, that this is what Saul was going to do. Then David followed up by asking if the people that he had just rescued would then hand him over to Saul. Again, the Lord said that they would. So, David left the area. When Saul heard that David had left Keilah, then he did not go there. In the end, the whole scenario never happened. God had spoken to David about what **would** happen, if David made the decision to stay in the city. God was speaking with certainty about a future possibility (the people giving David to Saul), even though it would actually never happen.[3]

The New Testament also gives us an example. In Matthew 11:20-24, Jesus rebukes a number of cities, saying that if the miracles that He had done in them had been done elsewhere, those other cities would have repented long before that point. Those cities did not have those works done in them, but Jesus knew what would have happened if they had. Therefore, God knows, not just what will happen, but what would happen under any given circumstance.

Some would object that if God knows the future, and He created everything, then He is creating all the circumstances that lead to that future being realized. Therefore, He is actively ordaining all the evil that happens. When He created the world, foreseeing all that was going to happen, by then creating the world, He was thus causing it to happen. This would be the case if free will were not an actual choice. If people would always respond to given inputs with fixed outputs, you could make that assumption. However, Scripture indicates that this is not the case and, as stated in the prior chapter, we know intuitively that we do make free will choices. In fact, I believe that this is one of the ways in which we are made in the image of God, who Himself has free will.

God certainly could have created creatures without free will. That would have been his prerogative. He could have done so, but Scripture indicates that, at least with regards to humanity, He did not. That is to say nothing about the angels, but looking at them is far beyond the scope of this book. If God did not create beings that are free to choose, then He could not have beings that are free to love, at least in the same sense of the word that we are accustomed to. Love is expressed through choice – free to choose and to show affection.

You can program a computer to say all kinds of nice things to you. People have made websites that you can visit that will give you an encouraging word. This may be well and good, but we would not call it love. At least, we would never say that the computer loves us. Some might go as far as to say that the programmer acted out of love, because he wanted to encourage other people, but we would never go as far as to say the computer did it. Why not? Because it had no choice. It had no feelings. There was no deliberation. Because of this, we would never attribute love to the computer. Rather, it was just programmed to behave in a certain way. God could have made us perfectly obedient, without free will, but then we could never have loved, or at least not in the same sense that we mean love today. It would be something different, but not what we know as love.

God is love (1 Jn. 4:16). The two great commandments are to love the Lord and to love our neighbor (Mark 12:29-31). Love is central to God. It expresses His very nature and what He wants from us. If God wanted to create a being that could understand Him in some sense, that could echo this love, then He would need to create a being with the ability to choose. It could not simply behave as it was hard-wired to do and know the reality of love. If God has a free will, could He not also create creatures in His image that also have free will?

When we speak of true love, we are speaking of something much deeper than just a pre-programmed response. It must involve some sense of care, of concern – a depth of emotion. Unless we have choice, this all goes away; we would become beings destined to behave in certain ways. God could have created such a world, but then how could He have displayed His love, mercy and grace? The world would be a very cold place indeed. This is not the God we see in Scripture. Rather, we see the creator God who created a beautiful paradise, set man in it, and allowed him to freely choose good or bad. Then when man chose to disobey, He sent His Son Jesus to be the sacrifice that would redeem humanity. This is love divine, all loves excelling!

So we are left with this: God knows the future, not just because He sees it beforehand, but also in the sense that it is to Him as the present. Yet we also see that although He knows the future, He has not forcibly caused everything to be. Now, in a certain sense, yes, God is the ultimate cause in that He did create everything, including freewill creatures. If God wants to create beings who are free to choose or reject Him and also create a universe with consequences, is that not His prerogative? Paul effectively says the same thing in Romans chapter 9. Who are we to argue with God? Job tried that before and found out that it was not a very good idea (Job 42:1-6). I am not sure what answer a mortal man could ever give when God asks, "Where were you when I laid the foundation of the earth? Tell me, if you have understanding" (Job 38:4).

Let us now consider the thought of knowing something beforehand, and yet not being the direct cause of it… In our own experience, there are perfectly natural examples when we can know something will happen before it does, but we have not caused it. If you are flying at a high altitude, you may see that a train is about to collide with a car. You know for certainty that it will happen, but you have not caused it.

There is also the more natural sense in that we may know things will happen without being the cause of them. When my family was serving as missionaries in Cameroon, there was a particular kind of hard candy that my wife really liked. It was like a hard caramel, except instead of being caramel-flavored, it was coffee-flavored. We would often keep some of them around the house, in addition to some of the hard caramels. If I were to offer my wife a choice between the caramel or the coffee candy, I was 100% confident that she would choose the coffee candy. I would not have had to suggest that she choose a certain candy, or coerce her. I knew what she would choose because I knew my wife.

Now, I am just a man and only have limited knowledge. As we noted earlier, God's foreknowledge is not like that, in the sense that it is far superior, as He is not bound by time in the same way that we are. However, the same holds true that He need not force us to make a decision in order to know what we will do. He knows what we will choose, even when we do not know. However, the choices that we face are real choices. We are making them, and we are responsible for them.

Certainly, God could intervene to keep free will choices from happening, and we do see this in the Scripture many times. God is inserting Himself into time regularly, and certainly in the most prominent way at the incarnation, when He stepped down into time and became a man. This occurs many times, whether we perceive it or not, when the Holy Spirit is at work in our hearts and lives, bringing grace, conviction and power.

As we stated at the beginning of this chapter, whatever happens, happens because God has permitted it. He ordains rulers. He raises up people and brings His will to pass. We will consider many scriptural examples of this in the next chapter, when we consider how free will mixes with sovereignty to produce the beautiful tapestry that God has ordained. People may try to challenge the authority of God, but His plans will never ultimately be thwarted. Rather, God ends up using the evil plans of the wicked to turn them into good. Some will object to this. They will think it very unfair that God would create a world with so much evil. But, remember, this is where free will comes in.

What if God wanted to create free-willed beings who would make very real choices and thus could truly know what it means to love and be loved? Some may not like this and may object to what God has done. However, we are really in no position to do that. Romans 9 has quite a lot to say about this. Paul asks, *"But who are you, O man, to answer back to God? Will what is molded say to its molder, 'Why have you made me like this?' Has the potter no right over the clay, to make out of the same lump one vessel for honorable use and another for dishonorable use?"* (vs. 20-21).

We may not know all the reasons why God did this, for who can fully comprehend the wisdom of God? However, again in Romans 9, we find Paul asking the question, *"What if God, desiring to show his wrath and to make known his power, has endured with much patience vessels of wrath prepared for destruction, in order to make known the riches of his glory for vessels of mercy, which he has prepared beforehand for glory"* (vs. 22-23). In the wisdom of God, He chose to create mankind, who would rebel against Him not once, not twice, but consistently. Through this, He will show forth His mercy in calling out to the rebellious and saving as many as come to Him (cf. Jn. 6:37).

If people want to still complain that this is unfair, we may ask – to whom is it unfair? If we look at the scenario from God's eyes, we have to remember the tremendous price that He has paid to have it this way. As a parent, you love your children. However, we could never love our children as much as God loves us, who is in His very essence love. And yet, through the choice of allowing us freedom, He opened the door, fully knowing the reality that would come – His children, whom He loves so much, hating Him and hating each other. Imagine how it would make you feel if your one son killed your other, or if your daughters were treacherous to each other – O the pain that would go through your heart! Yet this is how God feels every day as the world that He has created hates Him and each other.

On top of this, God does not just tell us that He loves us, but He sent Jesus Christ to die in our stead. There is no greater love than to lay down your life for another (Jn. 15:13), and Christ did that for a world that had rejected Him and become His enemy (Rom. 5:6-10). Not many people die for those they love, but what about dying for those who hate you? This is love personified! This is what we find in Christ. When we all had gone our own way, through our free choices, God was never distant. Instead, He stepped into time, disrupted history forever and became our ever-living Savior! He paid a tremendous price for this, but He decided in his infinite wisdom that it was worth it.

Psalm 2 gives us a wonderful example of how God is sovereign in the earth. In this passage, you see that the nations of the world are conspiring against God's authority. The Lord asks why they are raging and plotting in vain. The thought that they could ever overthrow the Lord's plans is simply laughable. Yet they plot and scheme. However, the end is already secure. It has been written and shall be. Psalm 29:10 says, *"The LORD sits enthroned over the flood; the LORD sits enthroned as king forever."* (ESV).

Ephesians 1:11 says, *"In him we have obtained an inheritance, having been predestined according to the purpose of him who works all things according to the counsel of his will"* (ESV). All those in Christ have a sure and eternal inheritance that is prepared for them (1 Pet. 1:3-4). God **always has** and **always will have** a remnant of faithful people that will follow Him (cf. Rom. 11:1-5). During the time of the prophet Elijah, there was great persecution against the Lord's people, so much so that Elijah thought that he was the only true believer left. However, God always preserved a faithful remnant, and the wicked would never destroy it, though they tried. This much is sure.

God is sovereign and no one can ever thwart His plans. Scripture says of Christ that He holds all things together (Col. 1:17). He is actively sustaining all things in this creation. So, this is another guidepost that we have: God is sovereign. He sees all, knows all and is in control. If we want to assert man's free will, that is fine, but we cannot remove this stake: God is in control! This, too, is a guidepost that must stand firm: God is sovereign.

So, how can this be? If people have free will, how can God still be in control? How can these two things coexist? The next chapters will now explore this very concept. If God is sovereign and in control, then what role do our choices have?

---

[1] *The Epistle of Ignatius to the Magnesians.* Chapter VI.—Preserve harmony.

[2] I am not specifically advocating Molinism here as examining that school of thought goes beyond the scope of this book.

[3] Of course, God knew from the beginning that this would be the outcome. He knew the choice that David would make once he had received the warning from God. So, in this context and many others, God is not a distant ruler who has created the universe and then sits idly by, knowing what shall be and leaving it at that. Rather, He is actively intervening, bringing about all things according to the "counsel of His own will" (Eph. 1:11 KJV). However, Scripture shows that *the way* that God does this is by working through the free-will choices of His creatures.

MIXING SOVEREIGNTY WITH FREE WILL

Previously, we have seen that God is sovereign over creation, yet He also gives us free will. How do these work together? What happens if free-willed beings choose to do things that are against God's will? Is that even possible, if God is in control? Are not those things mutually exclusive? In other words, if a person does something against God's will, but God allowed it to happen, how can it truly be against His will?

I think some natural examples could help here. A teacher has an overall goal of causing her students to truly master a particular subject. She wants them all to graduate with honors. When she gives an exam, her stated goal is that they all pass. Now, it is fully within her power to just give them all a passing grade. However, if some of her students are not deserving of such a grade, she will instead fail them. Her stated purpose is for them all to pass; however, if she passed everyone without regard to the level of their knowledge, then she would not be fulfilling her overall goal of causing her students to truly master the subject. Thus, her stated immediate desire often has to give way to her ultimate goal—both for the students in front of her and the students who will come after.

Or consider a father. He naturally desires for his child to be successful. He has at least two overarching concerns for his child. He wants to protect the child from harm, and he wants to have the child grow up to be a fully functioning member of society. Sometimes, these goals come into conflict. As a parent, there are numerous times when you think it would be better for your child to make a different choice than he does, but you have to let him choose what you would not prefer, so that he will learn from that decision. Now, of course, there are limits on the freedom you give your child. You do not allow a toddler to play in the street just because he wants to. However, you give your children the opportunity of failure so that they can learn to use freedom responsibly.

God, too, does not give us limitless choices. There are limits to our freedom. First, we are limited physically. I am free to run, but I am not free to run 200 miles per hour. I do not have that ability. I am constrained by my physical body. Likewise, I am free to do good to others. However, I am not free to do either limitless good, or exclusively good, because I am constrained by my own natural inclinations to do wrong. This inclination to do wrong is what we call the sin nature, which we explore later in this book.

It is enough for us to see now that while God desires us all to be good and to live in fellowship with Him, He also desires that we choose Him freely. We see right from the beginning that God desired to give humanity that choice. In Genesis, God could have decided <u>not</u> to give us any choice. When He created Adam and Eve, He did not have to give them the ability to sin. He could have chosen to not create the tree of the Knowledge of Good and Evil. He could have chosen not to forbid it and thus preventing the temptation in the garden. All of those are possibilities. But they are not what God did.

Scripture gives us some instances where we see that people do things that are contrary to what God desires, and yet He uses these things to accomplish His ultimate purpose. As we looked at Romans chapter 9, we saw that Paul specifically mentioned how God raised up Pharaoh, who would resist Him (vs. 17-18). Yes, God deliberately set Pharaoh on the throne so that Pharaoh would resist Him. In so doing, God would display His power and bring judgment on the nation of Egypt that had cruelly enslaved His people. This passage in Romans chapter 9 is referring to Exodus chapter 9 and the surrounding passages. It would be helpful to look at the essence of the whole event to see how it fits together.

First, in the call that God gives to Moses at the burning bush, we see how God commissions Moses to go before Pharaoh to present Israel's petition (Ex. 3:18-22). He tells Moses right away that Pharaoh will not listen, unless forced. However, God promises that He will do miracles and only then will Pharaoh let the people go. The people will not leave empty-handed, but the Egyptians will give them a large bounty of goods.

So, at this juncture, we know that God desires to set His people free. He has heard their cry and is going to move on their behalf (Ex. 3:7-8). We also know that He has purposed that they will not leave empty-handed. Now, He could have just forced it to be this way. He could have miraculously given them gold, silver, cattle, etc. in a similar way to how He would later provide miraculously for their daily needs in the wilderness. However, this is not generally how God chooses to work. Instead, we find that He raises up a man, Pharaoh, who would oppose His stated purpose of setting His people free. In this way, God's goal of bringing His people out with great blessing is going to be fulfilled.

God is going to judge and bring low the nation of Egypt and its people (Ex. 12:12). To do this, He hand selects Pharaoh. Throughout the story of Exodus, as God is bringing judgments and Pharaoh is refusing to let the people go, Pharaoh's heart is being hardened. An important question is this: "How is his heart hardening?" Scripture phrases it a couple of different ways. There are times when the text clearly says that Pharaoh is the one who has hardened his own heart (Ex. 8:15, 8:32, 9:34). There are other times when God is specifically said to harden Pharaoh's heart (Ex. 9:12, 10:1, 10:20, 10:27, 11:10) and times where the text does not specifically say who did the hardening (Ex. 7:22, 8:19, 9:7).

Regardless of how that last group comes out, there are two things that are true: Pharaoh hardened his own heart and God hardened Pharaoh's heart. So, we can say this – God knew that Pharaoh would harden his heart and not let His people go. This was precisely why He raised Him up. Also, God indeed confirmed Pharaoh in this path and as time went on even actively hardened Pharaoh's heart so that he would continue on this course.

Scripture shows us that people make choices, but these are neither without God's foreknowledge, nor entirely without His operation. Not that He forces people to act in certain ways, but in that He reserves the prerogative to both give grace to repent or to harden a heart that has been rebelling against Him. He exercises this prerogative as He sees fit. To be clear, I am not proposing that God has ordained and actively operates through every evil deed. However, He does use the evil purposes of man and even redeems them for His purposes, as we shall consider later on.

When we consider this thought of God's hardening Pharaoh's heart, we should not think that God is in the habit of forcing otherwise moral people to be wicked; that is not what we see in Pharaoh. In Pharaoh, we see a cruel man who was killing innocent babies in order to prevent the children of Israel from becoming too powerful (Ex. 1). We also see a merciless man. When Moses first approached Pharaoh to have the children of Israel set free, instead of agreeing to their petition, he made their burden greater (Ex. 5). His statement was in essence, "If you do not like your present circumstances, you really will not like them now that you have asked for relief!"

This was the heart of Pharaoh – a man who was extremely hard-hearted and cruel. This is the man that God had raised up to be ruler in Egypt at this time and the one who would resist God, even against the advice of his counselors (Ex. 10:7). Pharaoh was already a hard-hearted man; then there came the point when God also hardened his heart. That is an important point, because we do not find in Scripture where God hardens people's hearts that are crying out for mercy. Rather, we find that God resists the proud, but gives grace to the humble (Pro. 18:12; Jam. 4:6; 1 Pet. 5:5).

Let us also consider Pilate. Here is a man who was raised up by God to be the Prefect of Judea at the time when Christ would be on trial. Jesus specifically says that Pilate was given this authority from above (cf. Jn. 19:11). He would be the one who would have to give the death sentence to the Son of God. And yet what can we say about Pilate? Little is known about his past life from the Gospels or ancient sources. We do find a little about him in the writings of both Josephus and Philo; both of them write of his being a cruel man.[4]

The Gospels do not have much to say about Pilate, except for short mentions in Luke 3, Luke 13, and at the crucifixion trials. The Luke 13 account does not tell us much, except it does tend to reinforce what we find from Josephus and Philo, in that Pilate mingled the blood of some Galileans with their sacrifices (vs. 1). This does not necessarily imply that he offered their blood as a sacrifice, but more likely that he had them slain in the temple while they were preparing their animal sacrifices and thus the blood was mingled. If nothing else, this demonstrates that Pilate did not respect Jewish customs or their sacred places, which is what we also find confirmed in the other sources.

Another thing of great importance is something that we see in the trial of Jesus. When Pilate is interrogating Jesus, Jesus notes that His kingdom is not of this world, but that He has come to bear witness to the truth (Jn. 18:33-37). Pilate famously replies, "What is truth?" (Jn. 18:38). This is important, because it illustrates that although Pilate was a man who had the power of life and death for accused prisoners, he had no real attachment to the truth. Truth is the basis for justice and without it you will get only capricious actions and expediency. The fact that Pilate had no affinity with truth is evident in his actions that followed.

Initially Pilate wanted to release Jesus and found no fault with Him (Jn. 18:38, 19:4; Lk. 23:4). He even knew that the Jews had delivered Jesus to him out of envy (Mt. 27:18-19). However, this was not enough for him – he also wanted to appease the people. When the crowd threatened Pilate with not being a friend of Caesar if he released Jesus, Pilate caved to the pressure and issued the death sentence (Jn. 19:12-16). Pilate sentenced Jesus to an excruciating death, even though he knew that Jesus was innocent. This was a grave injustice indeed!

There is one other important part of this story – the warning of Pilate's wife. As Pilate was about to pass judgment on Jesus, he received a warning from his wife, *"Have nothing to do with that righteous man, for I have suffered much because of him today in a dream."* (Mt. 27:19). This is an interesting point. It was the Father's will that Christ would go to the cross, yet God gave

Pilate's wife a dream that caused her to warn her husband to have nothing to do with Jesus, who was an innocent man.[5]

This is remarkable! As Jesus had said, His purpose in coming was to give His life as a ransom for many (Mk. 10:45). At the Garden of Gethsemane, He indicated that this was the cup that the Father had prepared for Him (Lk. 22:42; Jn. 18:11). The most significant purpose of the incarnation was the redemptive death of Christ. Christ had even indicated that it was specifically through the cross that He must die (Jn. 12:32-33). Therefore, God warned Pilate, through his wife, not to do the very thing that Christ had said must happen.

With this, we see that Pilate had free choice. He was warned not to have any part with condemning Christ, and yet he did not listen to the warning. Indeed, God had raised up this man, who did not care for truth or justice. In essence, he was the perfect person for this ignominious task. This man was willing to condemn someone whom he knew was only delivered to him because of envy. He heard his wife's warning, but he still proceeded to condemn the innocent Christ to a very painful and cruel death.

Pilate is not excused from his responsibility. God gave him the opportunity to choose another way, by sending his wife to warn him (along with the pleadings of conscience that would have told him that it is wrong to condemn an innocent man). However, God always knew what path Pilate would take. That is why He raised up such an unscrupulous man to hold this position. Thus the greatest injustice in all eternity was perpetrated. Christ, the sinless Lamb of God, was slain for the sinful world.

Yet God used this injustice to accomplish His divine plan. As Peter said to the Jews on the day of Pentecost, *"This Jesus, delivered up according to the definite plan and foreknowledge of God, you crucified and killed by the hands of lawless men"* (Acts 2:23 ESV). It was the Father's plan to deliver Christ up to wicked men, who would pass judgment on Him, so that He could ultimately save those wicked men or anyone else who would believe in Him (Jn. 3:16; 1 Tim. 1:15-16).

So, God uses the wicked to accomplish His purpose, even though He does not approve of their choices and even seeks at times to turn them from those choices. Nevertheless, He sees the end from the beginning. He raises up people to positions of power to accomplish His purpose, not because He forces them to behave in a certain way, but because He knows for certainty what they will do. In addition, as we saw with Pharaoh, there are times when He actively hardens people's hearts so that they will continue on a course that they have already chosen.

Let us look at another famous Biblical example: that of Joseph. Joseph was the eleventh son of Jacob, but the first son born by Jacob's most-beloved wife, Rachel. As such, Jacob loved Joseph exceedingly, more than any of his brothers. As can be imagined, Joseph's brothers were not pleased with this and thus hated their younger brother (Gen. 37:3-4). To make matters worse, Joseph had a dream that his brothers would bow before him and then told it to them. This incited their jealousy even more (Gen. 37:5-11).

The rest of Genesis 37 describes how, when the opportunity presented itself, Joseph's brothers got rid of him. First, they planned to kill him, but Reuben being the eldest and thus responsible for Joseph's safety, convinced the brothers to throw him into a pit instead. Reuben had intended to go back and rescue Joseph from the pit at a convenient time. However, the sovereignty of God intervened and while Reuben was away from the other brothers, a caravan of merchants passed by on their way to Egypt. Upon seeing the caravan, Joseph's brothers took him out of the pit and sold him to them as a slave.

After being taken to Egypt, Joseph was sold to a man named Potiphar. While a slave, Joseph was industrious and was given some measure of authority in the house by his master. Then one day when his master was away, Potiphar's wife tried to seduce Joseph, who fled, leaving his coat behind. Not pleased at being spurned, Potiphar's wife then wrongfully accused Joseph and he was thrown into prison. While he was there, he was again given some measure of authority and responsibility, this time by the keeper of the prison.

I think it is important for us to pause a moment and look at Joseph's life from his perspective. First, he is a young man who was given two dreams by God indicating that he was going to be in a position of authority over his brothers. He, perhaps unwisely, shared this information with his brothers who were jealous enough of him to kill him, but instead sold him into slavery. When tempted with sin, Joseph resisted. For his righteous stand, he was rewarded with prison – some reward! From his perspective, he could wonder about a lot of things – why had God brought him here? Why had God given him dreams if, instead of ruling over his brothers, he ended up in prison, falsely accused and separated from all those he loved? However, the next part of the story tells us one very important thing – somehow, through it all, Joseph never lost his faith in the sovereignty of God.

We see this later when Joseph was given the task of caring for Pharaoh's cup-bearer and baker, who had also been thrown into prison. One night, both men were given dreams which greatly disturbed them. When Joseph came to see them the next morning, each man told Joseph his dream. Joseph gave them the interpretation of their dreams, but did not take the credit for the interpretation, but rather gave the glory to God (Gen. 40:8). When we consider what we have just seen happen in Joseph's life, this is quite remarkable! We cannot forget that, in many ways, it was dreams that put Joseph in this mess to begin with. Furthermore, the dreams that Joseph had been given did not seem to be coming to pass.

He was given a dream of being a ruler in his family, and instead of seeing that happen, he was separated from his loved ones and sold into slavery – quite the opposite of being given authority! Then as if slavery was not bad enough, he was cast into prison, so that he was literally now in the lowest station of life – a criminal. Yet he did not reject God, nor did he disbelieve that God was in control. He also still believed that God gave dreams and that those dreams would come to pass. In such a situation, how many of us would not be tempted to say, "Where are those dreams that God gave me? I have not seen any of them come to pass, and I do not believe in dreams anymore!" But, this is not what Joseph did!

Instead, Joseph interpreted the dreams according to the inspiration that God gave him – he still believed! Joseph told the cup-bearer that he would be set free in three days and asked him to mention his name to Pharaoh so that he too could be released. The interpretations that Joseph gave came to pass, and the cup-bearer was restored to his former office in three days; however, he forgot Joseph (Gen. 40:23). Here again was a trial of faith, and yet in it, we see the awesome sovereignty of God.

We know the end of the story. We know what happened, but at the time, Joseph did not. He still had faith in God but did not know how this all was going to play out. Imagine if the cup-bearer had not forgotten Joseph. What if he had mentioned Joseph to Pharaoh and Pharaoh had released him immediately? What do we expect Joseph would have done? I think it highly likely that he would have returned to his father. In later chapters, you see how Joseph yearned for his father and his brothers, especially Benjamin. What was left for him in Egypt? However, God had a better plan in mind, and it was, in fact, the plan God had intended when He gave Joseph those dreams so many years ago.

It would be two full years after Joseph had interpreted the cup-bearer's dream before anything happened for Joseph (Gen. 41:1). We can only imagine how long those years must have seemed. Again, his hopes would have been raised – he had finally been able to speak to someone who could intercede on his behalf, but Pharaoh's cupbearer forgot Joseph. That is, he forgot Joseph until the appointed time. The time came when God was going to send bounty and then famine upon Egypt and He was going to warn Pharaoh of what He was about to do (Gen. 41:25). It was at this time that the cupbearer remembered Joseph and came to Pharaoh (Gen. 41:9-13). The cupbearer may have forgotten Joseph, but God did not and He was using the free-will choice of many to accomplish His purposes.

This is brought out more fully as the story continues. We see that Joseph, who again attributes to God the ability to interpret dreams (Gen. 41:16), gives Pharaoh what he was seeking. He interprets the dreams, is set free and raised up to be second-in-command of Egypt. This has to be one of the most radical transformations ever – from the rags and destitution of the prison, to the throne (Gen. 41:14)! Yet the point of this was not so much for Joseph as it was for another reason.

A famine was coming, and God gave Joseph the wisdom to store up grain for it. This preserved the lives of people throughout the whole area. When the famine continued for a prolonged period of time, even Joseph's brothers came down to Egypt to look for food. There is a lot more to the story, but the one part that will suffice for us here is when Joseph revealed himself to his brothers. At this time, he said to them, *"And now do not be distressed or angry with yourselves because you sold me here, for God sent me before you to preserve life"* (Gen. 45:5 ESV).

It was in the plan of God that Joseph was sent to Egypt. Now, it is a remarkable thing that Joseph uses the word "sent", because being sold as a slave is not usually how we would describe "sending". However, it was the way that God used to send Joseph to Egypt. As we compare this with what Joseph said a little later in his life about this incident, we see something else very interesting.

In Genesis 50:20, we find: *"But as for you, ye thought evil against me; but God meant it unto good, to bring to pass, as it is this day, to save much people alive."* This is a very interesting point when we consider the sovereignty of God mixed with the free will of man. God did not force the brothers to sell Joseph into slavery. Neither did the brothers think that they were doing something that would enable Joseph to be successful. They meant it for evil. They seriously meant to hurt Joseph, but God used their evil intentions to ultimately promote Joseph.

In fact, when we look at the story with the perspective of hind-sight, it would be hard to see how this would have been accomplished any other way. God raised Joseph up to be the ruler, not so much for his sake as it was for the preservation of many other people. Also, God had long ago told Abraham that his descendants would go down into Egypt (Gen. 15:13-14). God accomplished all of this by turning the evil intentions that Joseph's brothers had toward Joseph into good.

Let us consider another way to look at the subject of God using the free choices of an individual to accomplish His purposes. Suppose you have two countries that are at war. Country A decides that it is going to launch a surprise attack against a particular location in Country B. Now, Country B learns of these plans in advance. While Country B cannot prevent the attack from taking place, what it can do is prepare to use that attack for its own advantage. It may set up a surprise itself so that Country A's attack will fail. It may also use the knowledge that the enemy's forces will be otherwise engaged, so it can get a victory elsewhere. In short, Country B uses the plans of Country A to accomplish its own purposes.

In all of these cases, Country B did not force Country A to attack. Country A chose to do it, and Country B, through its advanced knowledge used that information to ultimately work out something that was better for itself. This is a simple analogy (although it only goes so far) of how God can use the choices of individuals, even when they choose to do things that are not in accordance with His desires, to work out something that He uses for good.

God would certainly prefer that all would come to repentance. He would prefer that people were not His enemies. He would prefer that they did not sin, and yet He chooses to give them free-will. But, their free-will will never thwart the ultimate plans of God, because His plans are certain. Instead, all their railing and accusation and assaults only end up furthering God's ultimate purpose. He does not force the nation to do the attack, but when they do it (for God knows with certainty not just what someone intends to do, but whether or not they will actually do it), He will use that to fulfill His eternal purpose. You can never fight against God and actually win!

This does not mean that God has predetermined that people make those wrong choices. God does not want people to do evil things; however, if people are fully committed to doing evil, is it not within His right to somehow redeem some of that for good? Certainly, God (being loving, kind and good) would rather choose another path, but to do so would violate the free will that He has given to His creatures. Now, it is certainly God's prerogative to do that, if that is His desire, but consider the following.

If a person wants to do something that is evil, God essentially has three options:

1. He can let that person do what he wants and the evil happens.

2. He can forcibly change the person's mind and the evil does not happen.

3. He can change the circumstances so that either the person changes his mind, or the opportunity to accomplish the evil desire never materializes and so the evil does not happen.

Generally, we do not like the first option. We would prefer that God does not allow the evil to happen. But, as we shall consider later, if God stopped every evil from happening, it would cause some major problems. That is not to say that God never stops the evil by using option 2 or 3. I believe He does so many times, probably too numerous for us to possibly count. However, if He is the Sovereign over creation, is it not His right to sometimes allow option 1? Can He not choose to allow a person to do a wicked deed, and, in allowing it, though not condoning it, can He not then redeem it somehow and still bring out some good from it?

Indeed, for those who love God and are called according to His purpose, He does exactly this (Rom. 8:28). He redeems even the most horrible things so that, while He never approves of them and never desired that they happen, He will still bring out something eternally good from them.

---

[4] Philo of Alexandria, *The embassy to Gaius*. 299-305; Flavius Josephus, *Jewish Antiquities*. 18.55-59

[5] Some may object that Scripture does not say that God gave Pilate's wife that dream. That is true – it does not directly say it, although it is hard to arrive at another source. The context and timing would necessitate an origin from something other than simply a chance, natural event. The details of Jesus being innocent, etc., imply far more than what would just happen naturally. It certainly was not the devil, as he had just entered into Judas to bring Christ exactly to this point. It certainly then points to God's actively giving the dream (although, the main point would still remain, even if we were just to say that God only allowed the dream to happen).

GOD DETERMINES AND MAN CHOOSES

God determines. He has a master plan that He is fulfilling. However, that plan involves people. If we say that God does not force people to behave in a certain way, then what happens if people do not want to do what God wants them to do? How will His plan be certain if it depends on the free will of individuals? What if those individuals do not follow what He desires?

The story of Esther should help us here. In it, we see that God raised Esther to a position of influence for His people. However, in it we also see that while God's plan was to use Esther, He was not dependent upon her choices. Of course, God always fully knew what Esther's choices would be. They were never in doubt. However, from Esther's perspective, God's plan could be viewed as a contingency (for more on this, see the footnote after the section on Esther).

In considering Esther, we have another example of how God uses the free-will choices of individuals, but at the same time His purposes never fail. In Esther chapter 4, the Jews are faced with imminent destruction through the evil schemes of a man named Haman. Esther's uncle Mordecai was mourning at the entrance of the king's gate, and Esther, who does not appear to be aware of the problem, tries to discover what is troubling him. Mordecai sends back a reply to her, explaining the danger that her people are in and imploring her to intercede with the king on their behalf.

This puts Esther in somewhat of a quandary, because at this time the king is inside the inner court. Entering that court without being summoned by the king carried the sentence of death, unless the king happened to extend his golden scepter, showing his favor. The king had not shown Esther his favor by calling her into his presence for thirty days. Therefore, Esther faced the perils of either saying nothing and seeing what might happen to her and her people when the schemes of Haman came into fruition, or she could risk her life by going before the king when she had not been summoned to him. Both were extremely unpleasant choices which carried tremendous risks. When Esther explained all this to Mordecai, he sent the reply that is of most interest to the topic at-hand.

Mordecai tells Esther, *"Do not think to yourself that in the king's palace you will escape any more than all the other Jews. For if you keep silent at this time, relief and deliverance will rise for the Jews from another place, but you and your father's house will perish. And who knows whether you have not come to the kingdom for such a time as this?"* (Est. 4:13b-14 ESV).

Here, we find two important points. First, God will deliver His people. Even if Esther holds her peace, God is sovereign, and He will not allow His people to be destroyed. This is part of His eternal plan. Relief and deliverance will rise from another place for the Jews. In this way, God is completely sovereign and no one could ever disrupt His plans for His people. Second, we find that Esther's participation in the plan of God is based upon her willing obedience. She had a choice to make. If she kept silent, then she and her house would perish, but God would still spare His people.[6]

From this, we see what we have seen in other places – namely, that God's sovereign plan will come to pass and that He will use people to bring it about. He does not, however, use people against their will, forcing them to do exactly what He chooses. Instead, He pleads and reasons with them so that they might indeed choose the good. In fact, much deeper than that, there is the inner-working of the Holy Spirit, which we cannot see, that is drawing people's hearts to respond in the right way. The sad reality is that we often resist the Holy Spirit, even as the people of Israel often did throughout their history (Acts 7:51). The Lord works in people's hearts and certainly has the power to change them; however, people do have the power to resist that working of the Holy Spirit.

Some may contend that they would never assert that God forces people to make certain decisions. Instead, they argue that God, through the irresistible inner-workings of the Holy Spirit, changes their will so that they desire to do according to His perfect plan. Certainly, as we saw when we examined the story of Pharaoh, God does, at times, harden people's hearts. This could be described as changing Pharaoh's will. However, Pharaoh himself was also hardening his own heart. We also just noted from Acts 7:51 that it is possible to resist the Holy Spirit, just as Israel had done for centuries. We also saw earlier that God pleads with people to change their minds and repent. Jesus marveled at the unbelief and hardness of people's hearts. The fact that He marveled at these things is not consistent with the thought that He has either actively or passively *caused* their hearts and wills to be hardened.

Can God change a person's will? Absolutely. Is this the way that we *generally* find His dealings in Scripture? No, it is not. From the beginning, in the prophets, and continuing into the New Testament, we find that God pleads with His people to repent. Typically, He does not irresistibly change their wills to respond to Him. Certainly, it is appropriate to pray that God will lead a person to repentance (cf. Rom. 2:4). It is appropriate to pray that He intervene. If God can harden a heart, can He also soften it? Absolutely. However, to presume that this is what God is doing in all or most cases is going beyond what we find throughout the Scriptures.

Isaiah 10 gives us another example that provides some insight into how God's sovereignty and man's free-will intermingle. Verse 5 opens by saying, *"Ah, Assyria, the rod of my anger; the staff in their hands is my fury!"* (ESV). In this passage, we see that God specifically calls Assyria His rod – His instrument that He will use to accomplish His purposes. Then, in verse 6, God tells us that He is sending Assyria against a nation and people. Therefore, Assyria is a weapon that God has chosen and is sending to bring to pass His judgments.

However, in verse 7, we see how the Assyrians viewed this: *"But he does not so intend, and his heart does not so think; but it is in his heart to destroy, and to cut off nations not a few;"* (ESV). The Assyrians were acting according to their own desires. They had no idea that they were fulfilling God's purpose, nor did they intend to fulfill it. Rather, they were very pleased with destroying and plundering many nations. The passage continues by showing how the Assyrians had become lifted up in pride. They were boasting of their past successes and confident in future ones (Is. 10:8-11).

The Lord tells us in verse 12 that once He had accomplished His purposes, He would then punish the proud boasting of Assyria. He rhetorically asks if the axe should boast over the one who uses it, or if the saw should lift itself up against the lumberjack (Is. 10:15). How foolish this would be—for a tool to boast over the one who is using the tool! Yet this was what Assyria was doing. They were plundering and pillaging and were very delighted in all of this. They were confident that their tremendous success was because of their natural abilities and power. They went so far as to challenge the God of Israel, saying that they would do to Judah and their God just as they had to all the other nations and their gods.

God had indeed raised up Assyria to punish nations and to turn His people back to Himself. But, He did not pick a people and force them to pillage and fight against their will or natural inclination. Rather, He used people who were already so inclined to this kind of behavior – so much inclined that they were sure that they were doing all this by their own power. God then declared that because they had lifted themselves up against Him that they would be brought low (vs. 16-19). God used Assyria in the sense that He raised up a people who were wicked and full of cruelty. He ordained them to come to power and to do as they wanted to the nations. Yet in the end, they too would be brought low. God would not allow them to revel in their triumph.

Some may object that God would use the wicked to do such things. Does this not make Him complicit in their evil deeds? Again, this brings us back to the question of free will. If the Assyrians desired to do these kinds of things, should God allow them to do it? Would this not impugn the character of God?

If we say that God should have stopped the Assyrians from doing what was in their own hearts, we are saying that God should have stopped that evil from happening. This may sound well and good, but it leads to a problem. What kinds of evil should God stop? Should He stop *all* evil from happening? Where do you draw the line?

Suppose we consider the problem of traffic accidents. I think we would all be happy if God stopped all of them. We would think it wonderful if God would intervene and prevent the drunk driver from running the red light and hitting another car. The problem that results is when you take it further and ask about other violations that do not result in actual harm. For instance, suppose you are running late for work and you go through a red light so that you can make it to work on time. What would you think if God stopped your car right in front of the light so that you did not go through the intersection? Would you be pleased that He sovereignly intervened against your will to prevent you from running that red light?

Further, suppose that you expect that God would stop your car at a light each time you were going to injure someone, but that He would allow you to go through the light if no one would be harmed. In this way, God would stop the evil of your harming an innocent person. However, this would lead to absolute madness and take away all the real cause and effect that God has created in the world. It would lead you to simply speed to every red light as fast as possible, knowing that if anyone would actually get hurt, God would stop it before it happened. If you remove the effects, then you alter the choices that people will make and the world ceases to function as we know it. It would be a totally different kind of creation from what God has actually made.

What about the simpler choices that we make? For instance, if someone is borderline diabetic, should God prevent that person from eating anything with too much sugar that would harm him? Should God alter his desire to eat cake, so that he does not harm himself? If this diabetes is a condition that develops over the long-term, when does He start altering his desires? When does he intervene?

What about those of us who are overweight? Should God prevent us from eating donuts or chips? If He did so, would we not feel that our free-will had been violated? It may be God's prerogative to do that, but what would the world even look like under such circumstances? There is tremendous difficulty if we argue that God should stop evil from happening, because it then becomes nearly impossible to then say which evils He should stop and which He should allow. We are in effect usurping God's authority as the Sovereign of the universe. We are saying that we know how the universe should be ruled better than He does! When we set ourselves up as the arbiters of what should or should not be allowed by God, we are putting ourselves in a very dangerous place.

I do not for a moment mean to imply that God sits idly by and watches the world unfold. That is not what we find in Scripture. Rather, we find that He does intervene consistently in many different ways. He both warns people directly, and influences them secretly, of which they may be totally unaware. I am convinced that there are many times that we are saved from accidents and trouble that we will not even know about until eternity. However, if God were to totally remove human-caused suffering, to completely stop the wicked from doing any of the evil that they desire to do, He would be removing their free-will.

We find in Scripture this is not how God behaves. He influences and yes, even as in the case of Pharaoh, He hardens. He does not take the soft-hearted and make them hard, but rather, those who will not humbly yield to His plan, He still uses. He will allow them to go on as they wish, but in the end, they will find it fruitless and empty. Furthermore, they will end up furthering the purposes of God. We considered this when we saw how God worked through Pilate. God entreated him through his wife to not condemn Jesus, however, since Pilate would not listen, God used him to further the plan of salvation. He turns about the plans of the wicked to accomplish ultimate good.[7]

The question then comes, if God uses both the righteous and the wicked to fulfill His purposes, how can He then judge the wicked? Are they not simply both doing what He desires and ultimately fulfilling His will? Is there any difference between the two? Paul addresses this issue at least three different times in the book of Romans (3:5-8; 5:20–6:2; 9:18-24), and in a slightly different way each time. The objection could be phrased: "If my sin makes God appear more righteous, why am I judged?" or "If my sinful choices further God's plan, how can He hold that against me?"

Specifically, in chapter 9, after Paul talks about how God shows mercy as He desires and hardens whom He will, he expects the reader to object and ask the question, *Why does he still find fault? For who can resist his will?* (vs. 19 ESV). If the wicked are being used by God for His purposes, then why are they judged by Him? Are they not fulfilling His will? Paul's first response to this is that the potter has power over the clay, and who are we to argue over what God does? So, his first defense is that God is God and to argue with Him as a human is futile. What is the point in arguing with God, who Himself even gave you the ability to reason?

Paul does not just leave it there. He goes on to show that God's wisdom is immense. What if God is patiently enduring the wicked so that He can make His glory known in His dealings with those to whom He shows mercy, both the Jews and the Gentiles (cf. vs. 22-24)? If God endures the wicked, and rightly pours out His anger on them because of the evil choices that they have made, and then through His mercy saves those who believe in Him, is that not His prerogative? Although all people deserve death, if God wants to show mercy by granting life to as many as will humbly trust in Him, can He not do that?

One more thing to note from this passage, that we will expand on later, is that being born a Gentile and thus being born outside of the promises of God, **did not** mean you had to remain that way. God was calling both Jews and Gentiles together into a new people. Being born a vessel of wrath did not mean that you had to remain a vessel of wrath – rather God, through Christ, provided a way to repent. Though as a Gentile, you were rightly being called a child of wrath (Eph. 2:1-3), this did not mean that you were predestined to be a vessel of wrath forever, with no hope of being saved. Your destiny was not fixed. The apostles went throughout the world, preaching Christ and *"to all who did receive him, who believed in his name, he gave the right to become children of God"* (Jn. 1:12 ESV).

Before we close this chapter, we will end with one more example of how God uses the wicked to accomplish His purposes. We saw this earlier when we looked at the story of Joseph. The brothers, in selling Joseph into slavery, thought to do evil to him, but God meant it for good. So, even though God used the wickedness of the brothers, you could say that He actually <u>did</u> thwart their plans, because what happened in the end was the opposite of what the brothers had intended. They wanted to bring Joseph down and forever get rid of him. Instead, God used their evil plans to raise Joseph up. The very opposite of what they had intended actually came to pass.

In fact, God even orchestrated how it happened, having a caravan pass by at the right time and making sure that Reuben was not around when it happened. The wicked brothers had their plans, but God turned them upside down, in order for His will to be accomplished.

Moreover, in the end, even the wicked brothers were redeemed. When Joseph later put them to the test, we see the tremendous heart change that they had undergone. God worked it all for good. Sometimes we see this happen in our own lives and we can understand at the end what God was doing. Many times, however, we will not understand. It is in those times, when our faith is tested, that we must trust the heart of God, knowing that His plan is perfect.

---

[6] As we said earlier, this is not truly a contingency (unforeseen event or circumstance), because God knew from the very beginning the choice that Esther would make. However, from our perspective, it functions as a contingency. This is because it is a real choice. As we explored earlier, the fact that we know what a person will choose does not mean that the choice is not real. Likewise, God had elected Esther to be the person through whom He would save His

people. He always knew that she would perform that function. However, if she had chosen otherwise, God would have known beforehand that that was what she would do and would have already had another vessel prepared. In this way, from our perspective, being bound by time, the choice appears as a contingency even though from God's perspective the future is as clear as the past. Remember what we looked at before – God knows not only what will happen, but what would happen in any given situation. Therefore, a contingency for us is, for Him, a reality that could exist but never will. He can speak with certainty about it, knowing what **could** happen, but also fully-knowing whether it actually **will** happen.

[7] When we are considering the sovereignty of God, and this subject of Pilate, let us not forget that while God did warn Pilate, it does not mean that God did everything He could to prevent Pilate from condemning Christ. Consider how the Gospels tell us that Jesus did not defend Himself before Pilate (Mt. 27:12-14; Mk. 15:3-5; Jn. 19:7-10). Had Pilate known with certainty that the Man in front of him was the Son of God, he would doubtless not have crucified Him (1 Cor. 2:8). Although God warns the wicked from their way, He is in no way obligated to do **everything** within His power to turn them from that path (if even using the phrase "*everything within His power*" would be appropriate for a Being of infinite power!). This is precisely where the sovereignty of God comes in. It is God that chooses how much light to give to people.

ELECTION

We now come to the subject of election, which is closely related to predestination. We began the book by mentioning the terms "destiny" or "fate". We said that these concepts exist in some form in almost every culture and we explored the concepts of free will and God's sovereignty. We stated that we are free to make real choices and yet all of our choices, although often not preferred by God, will still be used by Him to weave the tapestry of life. This brings us to the Biblical doctrine of election.

Election is basically making a choice. In modern times, when an individual is elected, it means they are chosen by the people to serve in a particular capacity. When we are speaking of the Biblical doctrine of election, it is much the same, except that we are speaking of God being the one who does the choosing. He is electing individuals, groups, nations, etc. to specific things.

There are three main ways that election is viewed. A simplistic summary of these three views could be:

1. Unconditional Election; God chooses individuals, not based on anything they have done or will do, but solely because of His sovereign decree.

2. Conditional Election; God chooses individuals based upon the response that He foreknows they will have to the Gospel.

3. Corporate Election; God selects a group, to which individuals can belong, and the individuals are elect based upon belonging to that group.

The first two of the views listed above are mutually exclusive. Election must be either conditional or unconditional. It obviously cannot be both at the same time. However, the third view of election (corporate election) could exist alongside either of the other two views. It is especially common to be held along with the second view (conditional election).

A typical passage used as a basis for the belief in unconditional election is Romans 9:10-16. In this passage, proponents of unconditional election would emphasize that God loved Jacob and hated Esau before either of them were born and had done anything good or bad.

Proponents of a conditional election would use a passage such as 1 Peter 1:1-2. They would emphasize that people are elect *"according to the foreknowledge of God the Father"*.

Proponents of the third view would generally also believe in the conditional election view, especially in the sense of God's choosing and raising up people to different roles. They would use many of the same passages as the first group, such as Romans 9, but understand them in a corporate, not individual sense. They would emphasize that the Church is chosen in Christ from verses such as Ephesians 1:3-4.

This kind of corporate election in the Old Testament was undoubtedly true. Israel was chosen as the people of God to show forth His praises. They were God's chosen people. This was not because they were a good people, but rather they were chosen because of God's love and the promise He had given to their forefathers (Deut. 7:6-8; 9:4-7). The nation of Israel was not chosen because they were going to be a faithful and obedient people. God tells them they were stubborn and rebellious and had been so since He had brought them out of Egypt. Yet God had sovereignly chosen them to be His special people to whom He would give the law and to whom the promises flowed.

This election of the nation of Israel, however, did not automatically mean that each individual Israelite was chosen. God had promised to bring them into the promised land, and yet so many in the wilderness were cut off for disobedience, rebellion and unbelief. An entire generation, save for Joshua and Caleb, was refused entry because of their unbelief (Heb. 3:17-19). Nevertheless, God did fulfill His promise to the nation in that their children entered in and inherited the land which He had promised to their forefathers. This theme of God fulfilling His promise to His people at large, even while many individuals go their own way and fail to enter in, is echoed throughout the entire Old Testament.

Paul begins Romans 9 along the same lines. He laments that so many of his countrymen had not received the gospel, but notes that the promises and the covenants were given to the Israelites (vs. 1-5). He then expects an objection to be that if the Jews were not receiving Christ, was this not a failure of God's promise? He answers this objection by stating: *"But it is not as though the word of God has failed. For not all who are descended from Israel belong to Israel, and not all are children of Abraham because they are his offspring, but "Through Isaac shall your offspring be named." This means that it is not the children of the flesh who are the children of God, but the children of the promise are counted as offspring."* (vs. 6-9).

Not all the Israelites received the promises. The promises were to the nation, so while being an Israelite meant they could be partakers of the covenant, yet so many, because of unbelief, did not enter in. This was a consistent theme in the New Testament period, as John the Baptist said to the people, *"Bear fruits in keeping with repentance. And do not begin to say to yourselves, 'We have Abraham as our father.' For I tell you, God is able from these stones to raise up children for Abraham."* (Lk. 3:8).

During Paul's time, when the majority of the Jews were rejecting their Messiah, did this mean that God's promises were of no effect? No, because the promise was not to each individual Israelite, just like it was not to each son of Abraham or each son of Isaac. Instead, God had chosen the nation as a whole to fulfill His divine purpose of being a light, but not all the individuals in Israel would fulfill that role. The corporate purpose for Israel was certain. Christ would come through the line of David. Even when things looked bleak and almost the entire line was eradicated, God was still in control (cf. 2 Ki. 11:1-3). However, individual Israelites had to walk in the covenant if they wanted to be full partakers of the blessings that were promised.

In the New Testament, we are God's chosen people. We are a peculiar nation (1 Pet. 2:9-10). We are a people that were not a people – a foolish nation or as the ESV says, "a nation of nobodies" (Rom. 10:19 from Deut. 32:21). Physically, we are not like the nations of the past because we do not have all that much in common. However, God has called us from every tribe and language and has joined us together as one body in Christ. He has elected us to be His special people that will bring His light to the world.

We are chosen from the beginning as a firstfruits (2 Th 2:13; 2 Ti. 1:9). A big part of the writings of the New Testament have to do with the fact that God had chosen to engraft the Gentiles from the beginning. It was not something that just happened when God did not know what else to do when Israel had crucified their Messiah. It was always a part of His divine plan that Jews and Gentiles should come together as one body, the Church (cf. Acts 15:14-18, Rom. 9:24-26, Rom. 10:12-21, Eph. 2:11-22).

Up to the time of Christ, the Gentiles at large would have been considered the vessels of wrath (Eph. 2:13). They were outside of the promises of God. They were the wicked whom God used, at times, to judge His people, the vessels of mercy. This is what we saw when considering Assyria in Isaiah chapter 10. However, Paul makes a strong point in Romans 9 and 10 that now the call is going out to not just the Jews, but the Gentiles as well. God was calling out a people from among all the earth and making a new people of God, not ordered according to nationality but according to faith in the God who has called them into the light (1 Pet. 2:7-10).

Applied in the context of individuals, this implies that there was a transition of some of the Gentiles from the point of being vessels of wrath to being vessels of mercy. Speaking to the Ephesian Christians, Paul says to them that they were, *"by nature children of wrath"* (2:3). They were dead in their sins, but now are saved by grace and alive in Christ (2:5). They had been children of wrath, cut off from the promises, but then were brought near by the blood of Christ (2:11-13).

If we consider individuals to be predestined from the very beginning, this passage does not make much sense. If the individual Gentile Christians had been predestined from the foundation of the world to be partakers of the promises of God, then in what sense were they ever truly children of wrath that were cut off from the promises? Instead, it would only be true that they had *appeared* to be strangers who had not yet had the plan of God revealed to them. In reality, they would have been the chosen individuals whom God had elected to save, they just did not know it yet. Under such a scenario, these individuals were always a part of the chosen people, for God had elected to save them before He had created them. This does not appear to agree with what Paul is saying.

Rather, if we consider this election, this calling out of a people to be corporate in nature, then we can understand that yes, all of us are by nature children of wrath. As Gentiles, the promises never were for us. We were strangers and aliens. However, in Christ, the plan of God to also save Gentiles was revealed. Before we were ever created, God had chosen the plan by which the Gentiles would become a part of His chosen people. Yet, individually, we were still strangers and alienated from the covenants, unless we responded to that call by faith. Although our response to the call was foreknown by God, it was not decided by God unilaterally. The choice was real.

Further, these verses seem to indicate a more corporate structure of the church. Paul says, "You were not a people, but now are a people" (cf. Rom. 9:25-26; 1 Pet. 2:10; Hos. 2:23). The Jews and the Gentiles are now joined as one body, with the division that separated them removed in Christ (Eph. 2:14-22). Now, the call is to all, both Jews and Gentiles, without distinction (Rom. 10:12-13). There is no difference.

In the Old Testament, Israel was chosen. The generation that God delivered from Egypt and led through the wilderness was chosen, yet not all inherited the land. They turned back through a lack of faith and rebelled in the wilderness. Hebrews specifically warns us not to follow their example in falling away (3:7-19). The whole generation was chosen, as the ones whom God had led by fire and by cloud, and yet individually, only Joshua and Caleb entered into the promised land.

In Numbers chapters 13 and 14, the children of Israel were at the edge of Canaan and Moses sent twelve men to spy out the land, Joshua and Caleb being among them. Ten of the spies came back with an "evil report" saying that the people of the land were too strong for them to overcome. Joshua and Caleb acknowledged the strength of the enemy, but also had faith that God was stronger. The entire congregation of Israel sided with the ten spies and that generation perished in the wilderness, with only their children being partakers of the promise. Because of unbelief and disobedience, although that generation was initially chosen, only two people entered in (Num. 14).

In this way, we can say that while the nation of Israel was chosen corporately, yet individually, there had to be a response to the call. Joshua and Caleb responded with faith, while the others responded with doubt and disobedience. Israel was the elect of God, but individually there had to be a response to that call. This was true throughout Israel's history in that the nation was chosen to be God's light, and yet there were often only a few individuals who actually answered that call.

One other point to see here in Numbers 14 regarding election is that God is still sovereign. It is true that the choices of the children of Israel caused most of the generation to fall in the wilderness. God had called them to enter the Promised Land, and they did not. Then at the end of that chapter, after God had declared that that generation would not enter the promised land, the people realized their mistake and decided that they would go into the land (vs. 39-45). This ended in an unmitigated disaster, as Israel was utterly defeated because God was not with them.

Although the Israelites had the power to choose to reject the promise of God, yet they did not have the power to accept it *whenever they saw fit*. God provided a time for them to receive that promise and enter in, but once they had rejected it, God in His sovereignty, decreed that they would not have the opportunity to enter in again. God had limited the day, as we read in Hebrews 3: *"Today, if you hear his voice"* (Heb. 3:7b).

God is gracious and extends His call to all. Yet it is within His own power as sovereign to set a limit to that call, especially to those who hear the call and consistently reject it. That is His prerogative. Therefore, we must be aware of the seriousness of rejecting His call. We are completely dependent upon His continuing to extend that hand of mercy. Indeed, in the New Testament, Paul specifically warns Gentile believers that if God could cut off His people Israel, that He would not spare Gentiles who do not continue to stand by faith (Rom. 11:17-24).

Now, while we have been discussing predominantly the corporate nature of election, this does not exclude individual election, especially election to service. God ordains individuals to perform a specific work, and this includes both the righteous and the wicked. God will elect both to perform whichever task needs to be accomplished. We have mentioned many of these before, so we will not go into these in detail. However, a few examples of God's choice (or election) are:

- ➢ Saul, as the first king of Israel (1 Sam. 10:1)
- ➢ David (2 Chr. 6:6, Ps. 89:3)
- ➢ The disciples (Lk. 6:13, Jn. 6:70, 15:16)
- ➢ Paul (Acts 22:14)

The Bible also has a number of examples of choosing the heathen for a purpose, although it is usually expressed in slightly different terms than the prior list:

- ➢ Pharaoh (Ex. 9:16, Rom. 9:17)
- ➢ Babylon (Hab. 1:5-6)
- ➢ Judas (Jn. 6:70)

God chooses people both for good and bad purposes. We may ask, "Does He choose them with reasons that are known only to Him, or does He reveal His reasons to us?" Of course, God does not reveal everything to us, for He sees what no man could ever see, and yet the Bible does give us some information. Paul writes in 2 Timothy: *"Now in a great house there are not only vessels of gold and silver but also of wood and clay, some for honorable use, some for dishonorable. Therefore, if anyone cleanses himself from what is dishonorable, he will be a vessel for honorable use, set apart as holy, useful to the master of the house, ready for every good work. So flee youthful passions and pursue righteousness, faith, love, and peace, along with those who call on the Lord from a pure heart."* (vs. 2:20-22 ESV)

Note Paul's language. It is the master of the house that is going to choose how to use the vessel, but Paul specifically states *"if anyone cleanses himself"* he will be fit for honorable use. Because of this, he exhorts Timothy to flee youthful lusts and to follow righteousness, etc. There is a responsibility of the vessel to cleanse itself. Now, it would be wrong to overemphasize this point and say that we are the sole ones responsible for our cleansing. There are many others verses that balance out this thought to show that we rely on the Holy Spirit for any cleansing. But, for this phrase to have any meaning, there must be a role that we have in cooperating with the Holy Spirit in cleansing ourselves.

If the vessel cleanses itself, it can be used for a good purpose. Either way, God will use the vessel – He may use it for a good purpose, or He may use it for a dishonorable purpose. We can either be precious china that the Lord has delight in, or we can be a garbage can. Both serve a purpose. We are not used by God according to His eternal decree that He made before the world was created, without any regard to our choices. Rather, it is according to His plan **and** how we respond to the grace that is offered through Christ. God will not be taken by surprise at our choices, for He has foreknown each event from the beginning. However, He has also not fixed our destiny in the sense that our choices have no effect.[8]

Now, I want to briefly move on to look at predestination. We said at the beginning of this chapter that predestination is very similar to election, and at times the thoughts are so intertwined that the ideas and scriptures surrounding them go together. Election is God making a choice. Predestination can most simply be defined as having a destiny that is fixed beforehand. You could speak of the predestination of individuals or nations, etc. Earlier in the book, we looked at the concept of free will. If we have freewill, how does the concept of predestination fit in? How can we talk about having a destiny? Does not having a destiny or pre-determined outcome imply that our ultimate destination is fixed beforehand and therefore negate the concept of free will? Yet Scripture clearly shows that we do have free will.

Should we throw out predestination altogether? Regardless of whether you might want to do that or not, it is not possible. Predestination is a doctrine that is clearly established in the Bible. (See Eph. 1:5, 11; Rom. 8:29-30; 1 Pet. 1:1-2.) It is a guidepost along our journey and is very closely related to God's sovereignty. But, if it is true that God has fixed each of our destinies in place before we were born (for this is a common understanding of predestination), then would that not totally negate all of which we before said about free will?

We saw when examining election, that corporately, the destinies are fixed. Israel would bring forth the Messiah, even though many individuals were going to be unfaithful to the covenant and outside the promises of God. In the New Testament, the Church will be a triumphant Church, even though not all the individuals who are called will be a part of that heritage (cf. Mt. 16:17-19; 22:14; Rom. 10:18; 1 Tim. 2:4, 2 Pet. 3:9).

A number of people have used the analogy of an airplane.[9] If you want to go from New York to London, you would purchase a ticket to get on the plane. The plane's destination is fixed. It has been determined beforehand. As long as you get on that plane, you will end up in London. But, if you personally do not get on the plane, it will still end up in London. The plane's destination is fixed. Yours is only fixed to the extent that you agree to the terms and board and remain on the plane. If you do, your destination is perfectly tied in to that of the airplane and you will end up where it does.

In the same way, the Church has many glorious promises. It is the body of Christ, and we are predestined in Him to adoption and glory (Eph. 1:4-5, 9-14). We have obtained an inheritance in Christ, the down-payment of which we have now, with the fullness still yet to come. Since the destiny of the body of Christ is secure, as long as we are connected to

Christ, our destiny is also secure. It is not according to our will that this happens, but according to the good pleasure of His perfect will.

Adam Clarke writes the following in his commentary: "As the Jews were taken to be his peculiar people, not because they had any goodness or merit in themselves; so the Gentiles were called, not for any merit they had, but according to the good pleasure of his will; that is, according to his eternal benevolence, showing mercy and conferring privileges in this new creation, as he had done in the original creation; for as, in creating man, he drew every consideration from his own innate eternal benevolence, so now, in redeeming man, and sending the glad tidings of salvation both to the Jews and the Gentiles, [he] acted on the same principles, deriving all the reasons of his conduct from his own infinite goodness" (Eph. 1:5).[10]

What about verses that seem to say that God has specifically ordained individuals to either life or destruction? While we have already covered a number of such verses in their greater context, it would be valuable to look at a few more specifically here. In John 15:16 Jesus says, *"Ye have not chosen me, but I have chosen you, and ordained you, that ye should go and bring forth fruit, and that your fruit should remain: that whatsoever ye shall ask of the Father in my name, he may give it you."*

Some use this verse to support a view of predestination that is completely God's unilateral decision, before the foundation of the world. Certainly, this verse in isolation could mean that. Indeed, this verse does set a boundary that very clearly establishes that we are not entirely responsible for our own destiny. However, it does not remove the boundary that we have just seen that our responses also have a bearing upon our eternal destiny.

There is no question that it was Christ who called His disciples. He is the one that encountered each of them and called them out of their current situation to follow Him. He called not only the faithful eleven, but also the betrayer, Judas. Christ tells us that He called each of them, even though He knew one of them was not going to be a good follower of His (Jn. 6:70). Christ choosing the disciples was not necessarily a call to salvation, as is clearly seen by Judas being called the "son of destruction" (Jn. 17:12). Rather, this call was primarily a call to service. He had chosen the twelve, and each of them were given the opportunity to spend three and a half years walking with the Master. Yet one of them was indeed chosen for an ignoble purpose, in that from the beginning, Jesus knew he would be the one that would betray Him.

In the same way that Christ called His disciples, it is Christ that meets us and calls us out of our darkness. It was not the world that was seeking after God. It is God who in His love sent His Son into the darkness to redeem His enemies (Rom. 5:10). Still in our time, it is God that is drawing the world to Himself. It is the Lord that calls and draws us and it is our responsibility to respond to that call. We are not the sovereigns who decide when and how we will serve our Master. That boundary is also very clearly laid down in Scripture.

We find this in Acts 16:14: *"One who heard us was a woman named Lydia, from the city of Thyatira, a seller of purple goods, who was a worshiper of God. The Lord opened her heart to pay attention to what was said by Paul."* (ESV). This will be discussed later in the book, but we must be clear that we are dependent upon God to open our hearts. Our destiny is not all within our own control. Without God's gracious hand, we are hopelessly lost. That God allows us to participate in His plan is His prerogative, not an obligation.

Finally, let us consider Acts 13:48: *"And when the Gentiles heard this, they began rejoicing and glorifying the word of the Lord, and as many as were appointed to eternal life believed."* (ESV). Some use this verse to say that God has preselected some individuals to eternal life and others not so. However, we have already seen that our choices matter (Cf. 2 Tim. 2:20-22, Lk. 13:34, Jos. 24:15). The Greek word here for *"appointed"* can mean that God has caused something to happen, such as in Romans 13:1. It also has other uses such as in Acts 28:23 and 1 Corinthians 16:15. In these passages, it is man that is choosing or arranging the circumstances. In fact, this word in 1 Corinthians 16:15, which is there translated as "addicted" or "devoted", conveys the thought that they have set themselves on this course. They were predisposed to the service of the saints.

In much the same way, Acts 13:48 expresses the thought that those who were predisposed to eternal life believed. This is not saying that those particular converts were better than those who did not believe. Nor is it saying that there is something more worthy in them. Rather, in the context of verses 43-47, you see that initially both Jews and Gentile converts to Judaism were interested in hearing the Gospel. However, envy caused those Jews to reject and oppose the work of God, but the Gentile proselytes were ready to receive the new work. The Holy Spirit was at work (for without His work, none can truly repent and believe), but some were not prepared to receive the grace.

Verse 48 parallels very well with another verse in a later chapter of Acts: "*One who heard us was a woman named Lydia, from the city of Thyatira, a seller of purple goods, who was a worshiper of God. The Lord opened her heart to pay attention to what was said by Paul*" (16:14). It need not be talking about a fore-ordination from before time, but rather, when the Gospel was preached, the ground had already been prepared. God appointed them, opened their hearts, and they believed.

It is also not as though these Jews were predetermined by God to reject the message and the Gentiles were predetermined to accept it. Rather, just as in Acts 28:23-29, the Jews had hardened their hearts. They had been resisting the work of the Holy Spirit just as their fathers had done (Acts 7:51-53, Mt. 23:29-32). Certainly, there were Jews that believed the Gospel and were saved (Paul and all the apostles were Jews). However, the nation as a whole had hardened themselves, stopped their ears and would not listen anymore to what God was saying.

It is said of this group in Acts 13: "*But when the Jews saw the crowds, they were filled with jealousy and began to contradict what was spoken by Paul, reviling him*" (v. 45). They had grown calloused in their rebellion and when the truth of the Gospel came, they rejected it, as they had consistently **appointed** or **set** their hearts to do so through their constant rebellion. Envy at the Gentiles' coming into the kingdom consistently caused the Jews to stumble. The same Gospel that saved the Gentiles could have saved those Jews, but they closed their ears and God did not open them.

Before we end this section, I want to consider one more verse: *"For there are certain men crept in unawares, who were before of old ordained to this condemnation, ungodly men, turning the grace of our God into lasciviousness, and denying the only Lord God, and our Lord Jesus Christ."* (Jude 4). There are a number of ways that this verse could be interpreted. Some want to say that this verse is stating that people have been ordained to be false prophets – tares who will defile the Church. They were predestined to be wicked and thus judged.

Although, the verse itself tells us that their judgment was predetermined, it is not necessarily saying this of their actions. In other words, those who practice immorality and abuse the grace of God have long ago been appointed to judgment. That this is the main thrust of this verse is evident from the verses that follow, where the apostle gives numerous examples of those who did wickedly and are appointed to eternal judgment. He states as much in Jude 7, saying that Sodom and Gomorrah "serve as an example by undergoing a punishment of eternal fire."

The thrust of each of these examples is that there have always been apostates, but they are to serve as warnings to us. It is not something new. Judgment has been foretold to come upon the ungodly as far back as Enoch (Jude vs. 14-15). They are to serve as warnings to us, not because they were eternally predestined to be wicked and thus condemned to hell before from the foundation of the world, but rather, they serve as warnings because all the ungodly will be judged and this judgment is certain. As Peter says in a similar passage, *"Their condemnation from long ago is not idle, and their destruction is not asleep."* (2 Pet. 2:3). People are not fore-ordained from all eternity to do evil. Rather, the punishment of the wicked has been predetermined from eternity past.

---

[8] This brings up an interesting question: "How can something be foreknown by God, and yet still be a free choice?" This is not an easy question to answer, but I put forward the following for the reader to consider. Think about watching a recorded football game. When you first view it, you may wonder what the players are going to do. If you re-watch it many times, each time it will appear as if the players were each free to make their choices. You are removing the

actions from one time-continuum and into another. Existing outside of that time-continuum, you can stop and go back. You can fast forward. At each point, in reality, the players made real choices as to what they are going to do, but now you are viewing those choices outside of their original time sequence. You know exactly what those choices will be and no matter how many times you play it back, they are always the same.

Furthermore, if you wanted to edit something you could. From the outside, you could insert things into that football game and alter events. If God is outside of time, then the difficulty that many have struggled with regarding how God can absolutely know a future event and yet human beings be responsible for it is greatly alleviated. Of course, the universe is much more complicated than a recorded football game. Still, our God is just that much greater!

Now, one might object that if the players always make the same choices, in what sense are they free? I think the best way to think about this is that the future is free, but once a choice is made it becomes committed. If God is outside of time, He can see the future as if it were past, therefore, though the choices are free, from His perspective they are always fixed. This is because time is not actually ever rewound. The choices of the individual are not ever actually made again. Instead, you are viewing only a snapshot of a time-sequence, rather than an actual redo of the events. If you could rewind time with people actually making real choices (like in some movies), then you may see different results each time. However, that scenario exists only in the realm of science fiction.

[9] In particular, Dr. Leighton Flowers uses this analogy in a number of his Soteriology podcasts (www.youtube.com/user/MrLeightonFlowers).

[10] Clarke, Adam. *Adam Clarke's Commentary on the Bible*; Ephesians 1:5. e-Sword 12.2.0.

SIN NATURE

We are not sinners because we sin, but we sin because we are sinners. In other words, we are not born in a good state, with an inclination to do good things, nor in a neutral state equally inclined to choose either good or bad. Rather, we are born selfish and sinful – not initially in any acts, but in our very nature. When we commit sinful acts, it is because we are acting in accordance with the very nature with which we are born.

The Bible brings this concept out in quite a few places. We find that no one is righteous. We go astray from the womb, and have a desperately wicked heart (Ps. 51:5, 58:3; Jer. 17:9; Rom. 3:10). We also see that our natural mind is the enemy of God (Rom. 8:7-8). Throughout this chapter, we will explore the extent to which this sin nature pervades our being.

In the natural, we know it to be the case that we do not start out good. This does not mean that everything we do is bad, but rather that we do sinful things without needing anyone to teach us to do so. You do not have to teach your child to take something from someone else. Children take things from others by nature. They hit other children, unless you teach them to stop it. They lie to avoid the consequences of actions. You do not teach them to do that. You teach them to tell the truth. Yet they still tell lies and hit. They do the sinful things by nature.

There is a theological term that is often used to describe this natural condition in which we are born: *total depravity*. This term itself can be somewhat confusing at times, not only because some do not understand exactly what is meant by it, but also because there are groups that will each use the term, but mean something quite different. When I use the phrase "the total depravity of man", it would be helpful to have more context of what I mean by it.

First, saying that man is totally depraved **does not** mean that he is as bad as he could be. Also, it does not mean that he is so wicked that he never does anything that would be considered good. When people who are not familiar with the term first hear it, they may think, "I know that unredeemed people give money to the poor. How can we consider them totally depraved?" The point is that total depravity refers to the extent of the taint of sin within the heart, and that it is complete. There is no part of the heart that is untouched by sin's influence. So, it is not that unredeemed people never do anything good. Rather, it is simply that no matter what outward good they may do, it can never attain to anything that is truly pleasing to God. Nothing man does can ever be done to merit the grace of God or put a man in right standing with Him.

Second, total depravity is extensive enough that it takes the grace of God for us to come to Him at all. Some passages that illustrate this are John 6:44, *"No man can come to me, except the Father which hath sent me draw him: and I will raise him up at the last day."* (ESV); and Acts 16:14: *"And a certain woman named Lydia, a seller of purple, of the city of Thyatira, which worshipped God, heard us: whose heart the Lord opened, that she attended unto the things which were spoken of Paul."* (ESV)

In both of these passages, and many others, we see that it is the Lord that draws the sinner to Himself. The Father draws people to the Son. The Lord opened the heart of Lydia to receive the message of salvation. John 15:16 brings out a similar thought, where Jesus tells His disciples that they did not choose Him, but He chose them. This does not have to apply specifically to salvation (as we noted in the last chapter), but it does reinforce the idea that we are saved by grace (Eph. 2:8). We are saved because God chose us.

God sought us out. *"We love him, because he first loved us"* (1 Jn. 4:19 ESV). We respond to His love. We **do not** take the first step. No man can ever take the credit for coming to the Lord, for if He were not to draw us and open our spiritual ears to hear, we would not believe. Salvation is by grace through faith, from beginning to end.

Some may ask if we are not abrogating man's responsibility by saying that it is God that does the choosing and drawing. If God's drawing is such that each person whom He draws will irresistibly come, then this would indeed be a problem. This will be considered more in the next chapter when we consider the nature of grace.

Another important passage to consider when looking at this topic is Romans 5:12-21. When we say that mankind is totally depraved, we do not mean that he was always this way. In fact, He was created in a state of innocence and had no natural inclination to sin. However, when the first man, Adam, sinned, this brought tremendous hardship on the human race. From that point on, sin entered the world. All of us, as descendants of Adam, became sinners by nature, even as children.

It did not take long for man's sinful nature to show itself in a very open way. In Genesis, we read, *"The LORD saw that the wickedness of man was great in the earth, and that every intention of the thoughts of his heart was only evil continually."* (6:5 ESV). From the innocence of the garden, to the time of Noah, sin had fully corrupted the heart.

The passage in Romans chapter five is often considered to be one of the more difficult passages in the Bible. There are many different interpretations, specifically when you get into the finer details. However, there are two points that I think are pretty clear. First, Romans 5:12 says, *"Therefore, just as sin came into the world through one man, and death through sin, and so death spread to all men because all sinned."* (ESV) Sin entered the human race through Adam, but that sin did not remain alone. Like the spreading of a disease, the whole human race was infected. Adam sinned. Death was the result. Death spreads to all, because all sin. Adam sinned, and subsequently all of humanity sins. Death had begun in his body, as we read: *"in the day you eat thereof, you will die"* (Gen. 2:17 ESV). His very nature had changed. He was a sinner and so, we too all became sinners by nature.

Also, it seems as though there is some way in which the sin of Adam is imputed upon all of humanity. The exact specifics of how this works I think is difficult, but it does seem to be the case. For instance, *"Yet death reigned from Adam to Moses, even over those whose sinning was not like the transgression of Adam…"; "Therefore, as one trespass led to condemnation for all men…"* and *"For as by the one man's disobedience the many were made sinners…"* (vs. 14a, 18a, 19a). Each of these indicate that Adam's sin forever changed the relationship between God and man.

Some may object as to why it should be that we would be affected by the choices of another. Why should it be that Adam's choice would affect us? Why should we be counted as sinners because of another's sin? I think there are a number of ways that this could be evaluated, but I believe the most potent reason is what Paul was saying in the second part of the verses that we just listed above. Namely, that Adam *"was a type of the one who was to come"* (v. 14b ESV).

Just as we were made sinners through Adam's disobedience, *"so by the one man's obedience the many will be made righteous."* (v. 19b). By the same law of imputation, we sinned **in Adam** and we were made righteous **in Christ**, the Second Adam (also see 1 Cor. 15:21-22, 45). When we are in Christ, His righteousness is imputed to us. You could certainly make the argument that this is unjust. Why should we be credited as righteous? It is only by faith. If we do not like the idea that Adam's sin could be imputed to us, how could we like the idea that Christ's righteousness could be imputed to us?

The imputation of Adam's sin can be seen as a blessing, because it is by the same principle that Christ's righteousness could be imputed to us. We could have been sinners on our own, without Adam's help, but we never could have been righteous without Christ's help. Therefore, though this law of imputation may appear to be to our hurt, yet God uses it to impute the righteousness of Christ to us - a blessing more wonderful than could be adequately expressed!

Further, when considering the thought of how we could be treated as sinners in Adam, I think one of the clearest explanations would also be to consider God's foreknowledge. In the natural, we often judge a creature based upon the inherent nature that we know it possesses, even if that nature has never been displayed.

Consider the example of a lion cub. We do not put a little lion cub in a chicken coop with a bunch of chickens. Even if the lion cub had just been born and had never done anything to hurt another animal, we are sure that if we were to put the lion cub in with the chickens, it would kill them. It is a killer by nature. We would not put it in the coop and wonder, "Is that lion going to eat the chickens?" We know it would, even if it has never yet harmed any animal.

This is based only upon our limited knowledge of the nature of a lion. Yet remember that God has not only full knowledge of our nature, but also perfect foreknowledge of what we would actually do in future situations. Therefore, God can rightly judge a sinner based on his very sinful nature, even before it manifests. Also, eventually sin does always manifest in some way, in every person. This is why the Lord will at times take a person away before the temptation comes to which He knows they will fall. It is also a reason why the Lord encouraged us to pray: *"And lead us not into temptation, but deliver us from evil"* (Mt. 6:13 ESV).

"Adam, by disobedience, plunged this world into the slavery of sin. Jesus, by obedience, brought this world back to Himself. Because of what the first Adam did, we need to be saved. Because of what the Last Adam did, we may be saved. In order to be saved, we must be "in" the Last Adam."[11]

---

[11] Towns, Elmer (1987). *The Names of Jesus.* Accent Publications. p. 34

64

GRACE

We are saved by grace (Eph. 2:8-9). As we just saw in the previous chapter, we are sinners by nature and it is only by the grace of God that we are saved. No one is good enough to have merited the salvation of God. Furthermore, grace is essential for every aspect of our Christian life, from the beginning to the end. Salvation begins by grace and sanctification continues by grace (cf. Gal. 3:2-5). Jesus is the founder and perfecter of our faith (Heb. 12:2 ESV).

We are not saved because we deserve it. Indeed, when Christ died for us, we were the enemies of God (Rom. 5:8-10). Salvation is not earned, but rather it is freely given (Rom. 6:23). It was God who graciously sent His Son into the world to die for our sins (Jn. 3:16). Each of us separated ourselves from God by our sins, but the death of Christ has brought us near to God (Is. 59:2, Eph. 2:13). Jesus took our place, not because we deserved to be saved, but because of His great love.

The beauty of the gospel is that we were His enemies, unfit for the kingdom of God, and yet Christ died for us. He washes us and is transforming us into His image (Rom. 8:29-30). At the heart of this message is the fact that we deserve none of it. That is why the news is so amazing! We do not deserve any good treatment from God, and yet He adopts us into His family! It is all grace.

It is true that when people are compared with each other, some come out more favorably than others. Some people may appear more outwardly good. They may do many good things, while others are criminals. We saw in the prior chapter, however, that all are sinners. In fact, it does not matter how well or poorly I may compare to another human being. That is not the standard that I am being measured against. We are measured against the standard of God's perfect holiness, and in that light, we all stand condemned. It is only by grace that we are saved, not because we are better people.

Jesus' parable of the Pharisee and the tax collector illustrates our need to acknowledge that it is all of grace (Lk. 18:9-14). The Pharisee and the tax collector both went to the temple to pray. The Pharisee was very proud of himself, and thanked God that he was not like other sinful men, or especially this tax collector. He then proceeded to list the good things that He had done before God. The tax collector, on the other hand, would not even lift up his eyes toward heaven, but instead cried out to God for mercy. Jesus closes the parable with this statement: *"I tell you, this man went down to his house justified, rather than the other. For everyone who exalts himself will be humbled, but the one who humbles himself will be exalted"* (vs. 14).

Salvation is all of grace. The Pharisee was full of the sin of pride, and since he did not acknowledge his need for God, he could not go away justified. Tax collectors had the reputation throughout the Roman world of being cruel and greedy, and were hated by most of their fellow-countrymen. The Greek, Theocritus, when asked which of the wild beasts were the most cruel, answered: "Bears and lions, in the mountains; and Tax-Gatherers and calumniators, in cities."[12] This sentiment was especially true for the Jews, who resented Roman rule and considered the tax collectors to be traitors.

When Jesus chose the tax collector as an example, it was very deliberate. Contemporary wisdom was that the Pharisee was right before God and the tax collector was not. The Pharisee was revered as a holy man, and the tax collector despised. However, none of the outward righteousness of the Pharisee could save him. His prayers were not received by God. He was full of pride, not reliant on grace, and was not justified in the eyes of God. Meanwhile, the tax collector, who was indeed a sinner, went away justified, because in humility he fell on his face and pleaded to God for mercy. He relied on the grace of God.

At salvation, it is not we who chose God. He chose us. He loved us and sent His Son to be our Savior (1 Jn. 4:9-10). He chose us by His mercy and grace, not because of anything special that we have, or anything special that we will do in the future. It is all of grace. We simply respond to that grace.

Jesus tells us, *"I am the vine; you are the branches. Whoever abides in me and I in him, he it is that bears much fruit, for apart from me you can do nothing."* (Jn. 15:5). Without Jesus, we can do nothing. While this could be literal, such as without Christ we cannot even breathe, I do not think that is the main thrust of the statement. It is true that Christ upholds all things by the power of His Word, inasmuch that in Him we live and breathe and have our being (Acts 17:28). Our entire existence is only because of His grace. This is all true. Yet more to the point is that we can do no true good without the grace of God.

This Biblical truth has been echoed through the centuries. We owe the beginning of our existence to the grace of God and we owe our continued existence to the grace of God. Still more, do we owe the ability to think or do any good thing to the grace of God that enables us. When Arminius reflected on what St. Augustine said about John 15, he put it this way: "Christ does not say, without me ye can do but Little; neither does He say, without me ye can do any Arduous Thing, nor without me ye can do it with difficulty. But he says, without me ye can do Nothing! Nor does he say, without me ye cannot complete any thing; but without me ye can do Nothing."[13]

Calvinists and Arminians alike agree on these statements. In general, no matter your soteriological position, you believe in the necessity of grace for every part of life. The disagreement often comes, not at the extent to which grace is needed, nor at its transforming power, but rather at whether God allows this grace to be resisted or not. Calvinists believe that God's grace is given irresistibly, such that those to whom He gives it will inevitably respond. I believe in the ability to resist the grace for two primary reasons: I see it expressed in the Bible and without it human responsibility is eroded or even destroyed.

First, when I say that the resistibility of grace is found in the Scriptures, I do not just mean that there are specific instances where that is stated, although that is true. Acts 7:51 is one such scripture, where Stephen says to the Jews, *"you always resist the Holy Spirit. As your fathers did, so do you."* (ESV). However, there are many other passages that bring out this same thought: that people can hinder the grace of God.

The Apostle Paul warns about receiving the grace of God in vain (2 Cor. 6:1). If grace is an irresistible force that accomplishes what God has intended without any possibility of its being hindered, then how is it possible that it could be received in vain? If grace cannot be resisted, then it will accomplish everything for which it was intended and it will never be in vain. This view of grace makes this verse difficult, for it warns of precisely what irresistible grace would seem to deny.

We have before seen how powerful and necessary grace is for every good. Indeed, this is absolutely true. However, when God gives grace, He has also granted us the ability to resist it. Certainly, He could apply His grace in a way that we never could resist it. There are times when He in fact could do this. However, Scripture all too often shows us times where people are warned about resisting and failing and are shown to be tested by God.

Hebrews 12:15 warns us to *"See to it that no one fails to obtain the grace of God"* (ESV). If grace is irresistibly given to us without any human responsibility, how are we to "see to it"? How does that make sense? Earlier we mentioned how Jesus wept over Jerusalem and longed to gather them as a hen gathers her chicks under her wings, but they were not willing (Mt. 23:37-38). Jesus wanted to extend grace and mercy to them, but they refused.[14]

The theme of people's rejecting the counsel of God flows throughout Scripture. The Scribes and Pharisees *"rejected the purpose of God for themselves"* (Lk. 7:29-30 ESV). The Jews judged themselves unworthy of eternal life (Acts 13:46-47 ESV). Of Israel, God says, *"All day long I have held out my hands to a disobedient and contrary people."* (cf. Rom. 10:21; Is. 65:2-5). The Lord testified against Israel in Jeremiah 25:4, *"You have neither listened nor inclined your ears to hear, although the LORD persistently sent to you all his servants the prophets"* (ESV). In each of the times, the blame is always squarely placed upon man, because he would not listen. This in itself does not prove that grace is resistible. You could simply say that in none of these instances were the people given the grace to repent and change. However, that is neither stated nor implied in any of the texts. Instead, the implication is that the people, especially God's chosen people, could have done otherwise.

The clear implication of these texts is that God sent prophets and warnings, so that the people would repent, and yet they did not. To believe in irresistible grace is to say that although God sent the prophets and warned the people, what He never did do was to send the inward grace that would actually cause them to repent. He withheld the inner-grace that was actually necessary for them to repent. I agree with the Calvinists that without the inner grace, they never could have repented. The question is, was the grace withheld, or was it resisted?

Isaiah 5:1-7 helps us here. The Lord gives a parable about Judah and Israel and laments that they turned from righteousness to bring forth evil fruit. In the middle of the passage, the Lord asks the question, *"What more was there to do for my vineyard, that I have not done in it? When I looked for it to yield grapes, why did it yield wild grapes?"* (vs. 4 ESV). This is a rhetorical question where the Lord is saying that He had done everything that He could have done. He supplied everything that was necessary for Israel to repent and yet they did not.

However, if grace is irresistible, then the answer is very simple: God did not give them the grace. What more could He have done? He could have given them grace to repent. Because without fail, the grace would have been effective and incapable of being resisted. In order to hold to irresistible grace, we must believe that the reason why Israel did not repent and turn was not because God had done everything. Rather, it was because He withheld the **only thing** that would have not just **allowed** them to repent, but even **caused** them to repent.

This does not line up with the passage. Instead, if you hold to the fact that grace is resistible, you can say that God used every external and internal means necessary to bring about their repentance. However, the people refused the grace that was offered. It is true that both views acknowledge that God could have forcibly altered people's will, so that they would repent, but that He did not do it. However, which fits the tenor of the text better: "What more could I have done, except provide the irresistible grace that was the only thing that would have caused you to repent?" or "What more could I have done other than to have forced you to repent?"

Ultimately, God has the power to force people to repent, but we do not expect that He should be obligated to exercise that power. Earlier we considered the concept of what kind of a world we would have if God were to intervene and prevent all evil consequences from happening. We considered the topic of driving and how removing consequences would alter the choices to produce chaos. We also considered how love would lose its meaning as we know it, if choices were mere illusions. God could have made the world in any way that He desired, but He chose to create this world that we are in, with real choices and real consequences.

Scripture reveals a God who is offering saving grace to people, but proclaims that they are not turning to Him. It implies that they have a choice and that He operates by allowing that choice, within the bounds that He has prescribed. Scripture shows us that God is extending grace, calling and doing all He can to bring about the restoration of fallen humanity that is lost without His grace, short of forcibly altering their wills. While He has the prerogative to alter our wills, as the Sovereign Creator, he rarely does. Rather, Scripture shows us a God who pleads, contends and desires for us to be saved, and yet does not force us. This is what we see in Scripture.

In addition to the various Biblical reasons for believing in the resistibility of grace, we come to the logical implications that irresistible grace brings. Certainly, the most important reasons are the Biblical ones. However, the logical implications that follow from a belief and how that fits within the overall scriptural narrative are also important. This is particularly necessary to consider because the belief in irresistible grace is often paired with a belief in unconditional election, or the belief that individuals are unconditionally chosen for salvation.

These two beliefs fit together, and I am not aware of anyone that holds one without also holding the other. One reason, if not the chief reason, that these beliefs are held is so that all the glory may be given to God for our salvation. I believe this is a very good reason. I heartily agree that all the glory should be given to God. However, I do not find these two doctrines to be supported by the Biblical narrative and I believe they lead to the logical conclusion that God is the author of sin. I fully acknowledge that people who hold these beliefs do not come to this conclusion, but I cannot find a valid reason why it does not lead to it.

There are different views of how unconditional election and irresistible grace play out, but I think it is helpful to sketch out a form of the belief. Not all people who hold to these two beliefs do so in exactly the same way, but the following statements should describe the most important points accurately. There are some who will believe in an even harder line of predestination. I am choosing to include a softer form of predestination, because the difficulties that I am suggesting become only stronger as you move more toward a harder form. Unconditional election and irresistible grace paired together go something like this:

> Before the foundation of the world, God chose to create Adam and Eve in innocence, who would then fall into sin. God foreknowing (many would go as far as foreordaining) this fall, decided that He would save some individuals, but consign the rest of humanity to everlasting punishment. He chose, or elected, the individuals unconditionally, without respect to who they were or what they would do. God gave them grace, which they did not deserve and could not resist. This grace caused them to repent, turn from their sins, and be saved. The rest of humanity was not chosen by God for salvation, was never offered grace, and will receive punishment for their sins. This is all to the praise of His Majesty.

Of course, such a statement would indeed mean that salvation is completely unearned. However, it also abrogates any human responsibility at the same time. It has God fixing before time those who will be saved and those who will not, without considering any future actions or beliefs on the part of those who are so chosen. It is completely done according to the secret will of God. Those who sin do so because God ordained for them to walk in their sinful ways and refrained from giving them any grace which would have enabled them to be changed. Furthermore, it is purported that God receives glory from all of this.

It may be contended that those who sin do so by following their own sinful desires and so God is perfectly just in punishing them, because they are willfully choosing to sin. That is true. However, the issue with this line of reasoning is that when God created them, He had predestinated them to perform these deeds. Also, according to the Calvinist understanding, He did not do this because of His foreknowledge of who they were or what they would do, but simply by His sovereign decree. Under Calvinism, they were created for this destruction.

When John Calvin, from whom Calvinism gets its name, was writing about these issues, he stated: "But how it was ordained by the foreknowledge and decree of God what man's future was without God being implicated as associate in the fault as the author and approver of transgression, is clearly a secret so much excelling the insight of the human mind, that I am not ashamed to confess ignorance."[15]

Calvin expressed an appeal to mystery as to how God is not implicated in such a scheme. However, I do not believe Scripture leaves it up to mystery. Instead, I believe that it is clear that God has chosen to allow human freedom. He certainly foresaw the fall. He foreknew the actions of each person, and yes, knew that each sinful choice would take place. If you accept that God sovereignly decreed to allow human freedom, even if it be used for wicked means, then you have a way in which evil can be explained, without God being implicated.

Scripture teaches along these lines with verses such as James 1:13-15, which reads, *"Let no one say when he is tempted, "I am being tempted by God," for God cannot be tempted with evil, and he himself tempts no one. But each person is tempted when he is lured and enticed by his own desire. Then desire when it has conceived gives birth to sin, and sin when it is fully grown brings forth death."* (ESV).

A. W. Tozer put it this way: "God sovereignly decreed that man should be free to exercise moral choice, and man from the beginning has fulfilled that decree by making his choice between good and evil. When he chooses to do evil, he does not thereby countervail the sovereign will of God but fulfills it, inasmuch as the eternal decree decided not which choice the man should make but that he should be free to make it. If in His absolute freedom God has willed to give man limited freedom, who is there to stay His hand or say, 'What doest thou?' Man's will is free because God is sovereign. A God less than sovereign could not bestow moral freedom upon His creatures. He would be afraid to do so."[16]

---

[12] Clarke, Adam. *Adam Clarke 's Commentary on the Bible*; Matthew 5:46. e-Sword 12.2.0

[13] *Works of Arminius Volume 1*. Pages 384-385

[14] We see the contradiction between what Christ's expressed will is and what happens. Certainly, God could have gathered them anyway. He is not limited by free creatures in the sense that their will supersedes His own. However, He has chosen to limit things according to His own justice and with the accordance of His will. Christ could have gathered Jerusalem simply because He so desired. However, He chose to allow Jerusalem the freedom to reject Him, and responded accordingly. If God is the sole determiner of actions, He would be altering the choices of people to irresistibly accomplish precisely what He desires. If that were the case, then why would Jesus mourn over the choice that He had pre-determined to happen?

[15] Calvin, John. *Concerning the Eternal Predestination of God*. Page 124.

[16] Tozer , A.W., *The Knowledge of the Holy*, Chapter 22.

REPENTANCE

We have said that we are saved by grace through faith. Also, faith is necessary for every part of our Christian walk. Another essential element is repentance, which is something that seems to have gone out of favor in recent years. It is true that this subject of repentance has caused controversies over the years, and we want to examine it Biblically.

First, we have to note that repentance is not just something that is nice to have. It is an essential part of Christianity. It was at the heart of John the Baptist's message, as he prepared the way for Christ (Mk. 1:4; Lk. 3:7-17). Jesus, Himself, said that He came to call sinners to repentance (Lk. 5:32). Preaching repentance was one of the chief things with which Christ charged His disciples just before His ascension (Lk. 24:45-49).

Repentance was part of the core gospel message when the apostles were spreading the truth right from the beginning. We find that they preached repentance and its link to forgiveness and life. To cite only a few examples:

> *"Him hath God exalted with his right hand to be a Prince and a Saviour, for to give repentance to Israel, and forgiveness of sins"* (Acts 5:31).

> *"When they heard these things, they held their peace, and glorified God, saying, Then hath God also to the Gentiles granted repentance unto life"* (Acts 11:18).

> *"How I did not shrink from declaring to you anything that was profitable, and teaching you in public and from house to house, testifying both to Jews and to Greeks of repentance toward God and of faith in our Lord Jesus Christ"* (Acts 20:20-21).

One of the main Greek words that is translated as repentance is "metanoia". Joseph Thayer describes this word like this: *"a change of mind, as it appears to one who repents, of a purpose he has formed or of something he has done."*[17] To repent is to have a change of mind. It is to have a change of heart. It is to admit that those things that we once did, were not acceptable and that they no longer are to be condoned.

In Romans 6:20-23, Paul shows us the attitude of the early Christians. He notes how they were the servants of sin, but now, they are free from sin and are the servants of God. He asks them, *"But what fruit were you getting at that time from the things of which you are now ashamed? For the end of those things is death"* (vs. 21 ESV). There was and should be a certain shame at the way we used to be. Sinful ways lead to death.

The repentance that is embedded in the Christian message is an acknowledgment that our natural ways are sinful. It is an acceptance that those prior deeds are shameful. From there, we have the promise of hope in the Gospel that all those who believe have the promise of eternal life. Forgiveness becomes all the more powerful when we realize the depths of our sin and the truly amazing love of God that rescues the truly shameful and causes us to stand upright before Him, unashamed.

The preaching of repentance is something that is sorely lacking in our world today. It is sad that many churches and Christians seem to have either glossed over or completely rejected the need for repentance. Yet Hebrews tells us that it is one of the foundation stones or elementary doctrines of the Christian faith (Heb. 6:1). It seems to me that so many have been caught up in the modern anything-goes-mentality that a core element of the Christian faith is in danger of being lost.

The Reformation was a wonderful thing. It brought people back into many of the truths of God's Word. It restored many of the core beliefs of Christianity, especially the three solae: *"Sola scriptura, sola fide, sola gratia"* (by Scripture alone, by faith alone, by grace alone). Each of these major themes are the bedrock of Protestant belief. Many in the Reformation Era paid a tremendous price for these beliefs. They held on to them in spite of torture and death. We do well to remember them and not to let them slip.

With that being said, we must also remember that, in many ways, the chief errors of today are not the same as the errors of that era. The danger is in looking at some of the answers that were given at the time of the Reformation and missing the context in which they were given. It is not as though those answers are wrong (they certainly are not!), but they just might not be the right emphasis for today. People at the time of the Reformation were so used to the Catholic penance system, that their tendency to look for works and merit-based salvation was extremely high. The Reformers had to fight against this consistently, because this was the chief error of society all around them. This was the most common mindset of their world.

Today, the chief error of the populace at large is not in that they believe in the efficacy of works for salvation. Rather, it is more of a universalism, basically believing that everyone is pretty good in nature and that we are all going to make it to heaven—some just take one path and others another. Society at large has no general belief in penance, because what is done should be accepted as good, based simply on the fact that the person wants to do it.

There is a general disdain for anyone who speaks about absolute truth, especially if there is any hint of judgment in that statement. The greatest sin in such a context is the sin of telling anyone that what they are doing is wrong. This applies to the world and has influenced much of the Church, where the Church no longer preaches against sin, lest some be offended that the pastor was insinuating (or even outright stating!) that their lifestyle had to change.

Even though the primary wrong that the reformers had to address was not with a lack of repentance, yet still in their day, they had to contend with those who sought to remove the law and minimize repentance. There were those who were taking the truths of the Reformation to an unbiblical point. They taught that a Christian was not obligated to keep moral laws.

They minimized the role that repentance from dead works serves in a Christian's life. Luther was one who greatly emphasized grace. A key point of his ministry was justification by grace alone through faith alone. Yet he wrote against those who opposed any preaching of the law. He coined the term "antinomians" to describe those who espoused these beliefs. In a treatise against the antinomians, he wrote:

> *"Verily, I have taught and still teach, that sinners must be moved to Repentance by the preaching & pondering of the sufferings of Christ, that they may see how great the wrath of God is against sin: and that it cannot be otherwise expiated but by the death of the son of God: Which is not mine, but Bernard's doctrine. But why do I mention Bernard? It is the doctrine of the whole Christian world, and which all the Prophets and Apostles have delivered."*[18]

Today, if you tell someone that they do not have to work for their salvation, they will heartily agree. They never expected that they would have to work for their salvation. They always believed that they were good enough to go to heaven anyway. If they thought about God, they generally believed in a good God who would not send people to hell, except **maybe** someone like Hitler. They would consider it a great affront if you were to say that some of the things that they want to do should be restrained. Who do you think you are to tell them that something is wrong? They would insist that you cannot judge them and the Word of God should never be applied in a legalistic manner that implies **they** need to change.

This is the context in which we find ourselves today, at least in most of the Western world. We absolutely must hold to salvation by grace alone, through faith alone. We must hold to the sufficiency of Christ. We must hold to the supremacy of Scripture. But also, as the apostles did, we must hold to repentance. We hold to the sinner's need for a Savior. We hold to the cross, which shows the love of God for the sinner, but also the hatred of God for sin.

In the cross, we see both the love of God in wanting to save all men, but also His justice, in that He could not leave sin unpunished. Rather,

He Himself paid the price, *"…that whoever believes in him should not perish but have eternal life."* (Jn. 3:16 ESV). The holiness of God is displayed in the cross, in that God did not simply say, "You are all good enough and I will just accept you as you are." No! The Son of God suffered a cruel death, because our sin was so grievous, so abhorrent to God, that it could not just be excused. There was a cost for our sins.

In our day, there is a tendency to view sin as something that happens, but not being all that bad. If it were not "all that bad", then Jesus would not have had to die. If we were good enough on our own, and our own works were good enough for our salvation, *"…then Christ died for no purpose"* (Gal. 2:21 ESV). We must see sin how God does – as something that is truly repugnant and awful. It is something truly horrible. Then we remember the grace of God in Christ. We remember the love that He shows, when He promises to forgive us and *"though your sins are like scarlet, they shall be as white as snow"* (Is. 1:18 ESV). A proper understanding of sin gives us a proper understanding of the true grace and mercy that we have in Christ.

The Old Testament saints had a constant reminder of their sinfulness. They had to continually offer sacrifices when they sinned. Not that we want to go back to that by any means! Thank the Lord that we are delivered from that! The fact that we no longer need to be conscious of our past sins is a tremendous benefit of the New Covenant (Heb. 10:1-14). However, we should not fall into the trap of trivializing sin. Rather, we should remember the tremendous price that Jesus paid for our redemption. We should remember that while salvation is free to us, it was not free. It was bought by the tremendous price of the life of the Son of God.

Repentance is foundational to our Christian experience. It involves conviction. It is an acknowledgement of the truth. Our ways have not been correct. To truly repent is to neither fight nor deny that we have sinned and done wrong. It is when we repent and acknowledge our failures that the true cleansing happens. John tells us, *"If we confess our sins, he is faithful and just to forgive us our sins and to cleanse us from all unrighteousness.*

If we say we have not sinned, we make him a liar, and his word is not in us" (1 Jn. 1:9-10).

Of course, this is true at salvation, but it is also true as we continue in the Christian life. Repentance from our dead works is necessary to enter into salvation and it must continue. As John also says, *"But if we walk in the light, as he is in the light, we have fellowship with one another, and the blood of Jesus his Son cleanses us from all sin. If we say we have no sin, we deceive ourselves, and the truth is not in us"* (1 Jn. 1:7-8). Every one of us sins. Maybe not as much as we used to and hopefully not in the same ways that we used to. God is still working on us. John Newton is quoted as saying, "I am not what I ought to be, I am not what I want to be, I am not what I hope to be in another world; but still I am not what I once used to be, and by the grace of God I am what I am."

When we sin, we have a choice. We could just ignore it and pretend it did not happen. We could also say that we are loved and forgiven by God, so it is not important. Both of these actions miss the reality that our sins are deeply hurtful, not only in many cases to others, but to the God who created us. Instead, we should humbly confess our sins and admit that we have done wrong.

We have noted before that God desires those who have a humble heart (Mic. 6:8). A confession and renouncing of our sin is an important part of our continued journey of sanctification. Many times throughout Scripture we are exhorted to acknowledge our sins (cf. Jer. 3:13; Lev. 26:40-42; Job 33:27-28). When we confess that we have done wrong, it means we cannot just ignore the sin anymore. We cannot just pretend like it does not matter. Rather, we are acknowledging that this particular thing was sinful and that we are sorry for having done it.

There is a certain shame there, but with that shame also comes the certainty of forgiveness, knowing that Christ has paid the price and that in Him we are free from the sting of guilt. Note, we cannot and will not merit our forgiveness through repentance. Saying that we are sorry for our sin will never earn God's justification. However, crying out to God for mercy and cleansing is what we see throughout the Holy Scriptures. It is the one who says, *"God be merciful to me a sinner"* who leaves justified (cf. Lk. 18:9-14).

When we are talking about repentance after salvation here, I think it is important to note that we are talking about repenting for specific things. At salvation, we were justified and made right in His sight. It is not necessary for us to be saved all over again every time we sin. We are not talking about repenting for all our past deeds that were taken care of at the cross. Rather, this is concerning specific things that we have done and God is dealing with at the moment. Certainly, God can bring past things to our mind that indicate patterns of behavior that still need to be addressed in our lives. However, we also have to be careful not to dig up old sins that He has long ago forgotten and forgiven. This would be an imbalance in fully the other direction.

Here, I believe John chapter 13 helps us. The first fifteen verses give us the story of Jesus washing the disciple's feet at the Last Supper. He does this as an example of how we are to serve one another (vs. 14-15). But there is something else in this story that is also very important. We will focus specifically on verses 6-11:

> *He came to Simon Peter, who said to him, "Lord, do you wash my feet?" Jesus answered him, "What I am doing you do not understand now, but afterward you will understand." Peter said to him, "You shall never wash my feet." Jesus answered him, "If I do not wash you, you have no share with me." Simon Peter said to him, "Lord, not my feet only but also my hands and my head!" Jesus said to him, "The one who has bathed does not need to wash, except for his feet, but is completely clean. And you are clean, but not every one of you." For he knew who was to betray him; that was why he said, "Not all of you are clean." (ESV)*

Jesus used this washing of the feet as a metaphor for a spiritual cleansing. We see this from a few points in this passage. Particularly, in verse 8, Jesus tells Peter, *"If I do not wash you, you have no share with me."* Then, in verse 11, speaking of Judas, Jesus says, *"Not all of you are clean."* This foot washing therefore refers not to just how we are to serve one another, but also it shows our need for a spiritual cleansing.

This is, of course, a common theme of Scripture. Paul later echoes much of these same sentiments, when he says of Christ *"that he might sanctify her, having cleansed her by the washing of water with the word, so that he might present the church to himself in splendor, without spot or wrinkle or any such thing, that she might be holy and without blemish"* (Eph. 5:26-27 ESV). We certainly expect this to be true at salvation, but as we see in this passage in John, Jesus shows us that it is not something that is needed just once.

When Peter tried to resist letting Jesus wash his feet, he was rebuked. Then Peter flipped completely the opposite way and wanted to have his hands and head washed too, not just his feet. Jesus, again, corrected Peter with the words, *"The one who has bathed does not need to wash, except for his feet, but is completely clean. And you are clean, but not every one of you"* (v. 10a ESV).

The disciples, except Judas, were walking in the truth. They were walking with the Son of God. Judas, however, had already decided to betray Jesus (cf. Mt. 26:14-16). He was a thief and was stealing from the shared money bag (Jn. 12:4-6). Therefore, Judas was not clean. Though Jesus washed his feet, his heart was still desperately wicked. His hands that had stolen, and his head that had contrived to betray the Son of God, were by no means clean!

On the other hand, Peter was clean. Yet he still needed to have his feet washed. When we are saved, we are clean. We are washed, we are sanctified, we are justified in the name of the Lord Jesus (1 Cor. 6:11). However, we still need to have a perpetual cleaning. As we walk in this life, our feet get dusty. We do not walk perfectly. We stumble and fall. Then we come to Christ for the cleansing and we are completely clean again.

We do not have to get saved all over again. We do not need everything washed. However, there are specific things that we do need cleansed. As we walk this walk of faith, the Lord, by His Spirit, will put emphasis on things in our lives that need to change. He will point to areas where our walk is failing. He will show us things that need to be addressed. As He does, it is then that we confess our sin to our Heavenly High Priest. We bring it to the light. Then we are cleansed and we remain in constant fellowship with the Lord. This is a part of our daily communion with Him.

> *"But if we walk in the light, as he is in the light, we have fellowship with one another, and the blood of Jesus his Son cleanses us from all sin. If we say we have no sin, we deceive ourselves, and the truth is not in us. If we confess our sins, he is faithful and just to forgive us our sins and to cleanse us from all unrighteousness"* (1 Jn. 1:7-9).

Be honest with the Lord. If you have sinned, confess your sin. Take it to the One who sees all. Humbly repent at the foot of the cross and find the joy and peace that only He can bring. Hear the words of the prophet Hosea: *"Take with you words and return to the LORD; say to him, "Take away all iniquity; accept what is good, and we will pay with bulls the vows of our lips"* (Hos. 14:2 ESV).

---

[17] Thayer, Joseph, *Greek–English Lexicon of the New Testament*, 1886, 1889

[18] Luther, Martin. *A Treatise against Antinomians written in an Epistolary way, by D. Martin Luther, translated out of the high Dutch original; containing the mind of Luther against Antinomians and a recantation of John Agricola Eislebius their first father.* (accessed 9/20/20). https://www.truecovenanter.com/truelutheran/luther_against_the_antinomians.html

84

THE WALK OF FAITH

We have said that we are saved by grace through faith. This is how our Christian life begins. But, it is not just how it begins, but also how it continues. The Christian walk is a walk of faith. We are not meant to be a people who exclusively live our lives according to a strict set of outward rules. Rather, it is a walk of faith that is unique and personal. This does not mean that there are no guidelines and rules. In fact, God's Word very much must be the standard throughout our entire lives. However, our Christian life is not to become a life of precepts, lest it become a life where we approve of ourselves and disapprove of others.

Paul tells us: *"For I am not ashamed of the gospel, for it is the power of God for salvation to everyone who believes, to the Jew first and also to the Greek. For in it the righteousness of God is revealed from faith for faith, as it is written, 'The righteous shall live by faith'"* (Rom. 1:16-17). These verses, particularly verse 17, were probably the most important verses of the Reformation. The Gospel is the power of God for salvation to all who believe. In the Gospel, the righteousness of God is seen in Christ by faith and received by faith. The righteous live by faith. Yes, faith is the beginning of the journey, but it never ceases to be a part of our Christian life.

In this chapter, we will be particularly contrasting the walk of faith and the continued work of the Holy Spirit in our lives, with a life that is ruled solely by laws. The purpose of this is not to be anti-law (as discussed in the prior chapter), but rather it is to make it clear that in the Christian life, we are not primarily followers of rules, but followers of One. Remember, we do not serve simply an irresistible force. Rather, we serve a personal God, who loves, hates, laughs and cries. Therefore, our relationship with Him is much more than a simple sum of all our deeds.

Principles can be important. Having discipline in our lives is valuable in the sense that it can help to keep us from living in a careless fashion. However, we need to remember that the principles that we follow, or the discipline that we have in Bible reading or prayer, is not of itself merit-worthy. It does not make us any better than another. These are not the things that make us holy, although these things are important in the Christian life and are often a primary conduit that the Lord uses to change us.

When we are saved, we have said that it is by grace through faith. We are justified, or declared righteous, before God through faith in Christ (Rom. 5:1). At salvation, many things are changed. We are instantly translated from the power of darkness into the kingdom of light (Col. 1:13). We have a different ruler now and are not under bondage. We are adopted into the family of God (Rom. 8:16-17). We are now His. We are a new creation: the old has gone and the new has come (2 Cor. 3:18). We are born again (Jn. 3:3-5).

This does not mean, however, that our character will remain the same from the moment we are saved until the end of our Christian life. Rather, the Christian life is a life of growth and change. Our justification does not rest upon our works, but neither do our works remain the same as they were when we were first saved. Once we are saved, the Lord does not leave us as we are. At the moment of salvation, there are bondages that are broken. When people come to the Lord in repentance, sins are forgiven, and often there is a radical transformation of the life. However, there are still many vestiges of the old life that remain. The Lord deals with these as we yield to Him throughout our journey on this earth.

At salvation, yes, there is an instant change in the life, but that change is not complete. Paul says to the Philippians, *"And I am sure of this, that he who began a good work in you will bring it to completion at the day of Jesus Christ"* (Php. 1:6 ESV). The Lord began the good work in us at salvation, and He will continue to work in us, until the day of the Lord. As long as we are in this body, the Lord will continue to work in us, so that we might be more like Him. It is He that started the work in us, but His plan is not just to save us from the condemnation of hell, but to also transform us for His glory.

In another passage, right after Paul tells us that we are saved by grace through faith, without any possibility of boasting, he goes on to tell us that, *"…we are his workmanship, created in Christ Jesus for good works, which God prepared beforehand, that we should walk in them"* (Eph. 2:10). We are His work, His new creation. He has fashioned us for His glory and has ordained good works for us to walk in. The Bible specifically tells us that the will of God for us is our sanctification (1 Th. 4:3), for *"…God has not called us for impurity, but in holiness"* (1 Th. 4:7 ESV).

There is a doctrine going around in the church today that is dangerous, which we touched on in the prior chapter. This doctrine, which is very much a reflection of our culture, basically says, "Since I have been saved by faith in Christ, I am not under the law or any condemnation. Regardless of how I live, I am perfect in Christ." While this can sound spiritual, it is a horribly distorted message, and is faithful to neither the tenets of the Reformation nor the Biblical message. It is popular to many, because it essentially says that you get all the benefits of being in God's family without having to adopt any of His requirements.

While a central theme of the Reformation was salvation by faith alone, the Reformers were careful to never go into the above heresy. A thought that Luther, Calvin and others expressed is that while salvation is through faith alone, true faith never remains alone. Later, John Wesley's doctrine could be summed up as follows: "Salvation is by grace alone through faith alone, but true faith is never alone."[19] While it is true that we are justified and sanctified by grace through faith, genuine faith is living faith. Living faith requires action (Jam. 2:14-26).

If we look at salvation as a "get-out-of-jail-free" card, we are missing something. Salvation is to be all-encompassing. It is where the Lord starts a work in us and then works all the way through until the work is finished. It is instantaneous, whereby we are adopted into His family. Then it is continuous, whereby we are continually being saved (1 Cor. 1:18, 15:2; 2 Cor. 2:15). Ultimately, the work will be completed in us, when we finally see our Lord face to face. Until that time, we are being changed into His likeness, from glory to glory (2 Cor. 3:18). Our salvation is past, present and future.

Salvation is not just about rescuing us from hell. If that were all it were, that in itself would be amazing. However, Scripture tells us that it is much more than that. It is a salvation from our sins. It is a transformed life. It is the beginning of a relationship and a journey.

In his book *Mere Christianity*, C.S. Lewis illustrates the point quite poignantly.[20] In the chapter entitled "Counting the Cost", Lewis recounts how he used to have tooth aches as a child, but would not go to his mother for care right away. Instead, he would wait until it got quite unbearable. The chief reason he delayed was not because he expected no relief from his mother, but rather because he knew that she would not just give him temporary relief. Rather, after giving him something to quell the pain, she would also take him to the dentist. And this is what he feared. The dentist was not going to just fix the immediate problem, but also prod around and perhaps deal with things that Lewis had not even yet known were an issue.

This was going to be painful. Lewis wanted the immediate relief of his pain being taken away, but he was not interested in the other things that the dentist was going to do, because they were also going to be painful. Lewis says all of this in order to illustrate the point that God does not just take away our immediate pain. It is not only forgiveness of sins that He is interested in giving us. He is looking to transform our lives. He is looking to change us and once we receive His offer of salvation all the rest must come too. He is not interested in only fixing the tooth that is causing us the most pain, but God is interested in our long-term benefit and His glory. God is working all things together, that we might be conformed to the image of His Son, and be the sons and daughters that He has ordained us to be (cf. Rom. 8:28-30).

This present process of being saved and changed is called sanctification. The Lord is molding us for His glory. It is sometimes painful. It is His work, but as with our initial salvation, it requires us to yield to that work. Paul gives us an example of how these two have to work together in Philippians 2:12-13. In verse 12, he tells us to work out our own salvation with fear and trembling, following right up in verse 13 with telling us that it is God who is working in us to give us the desire and the ability to please Him.

From this passage and many others, there are two extremes that we want to avoid. We want to avoid having a careless attitude, whereby we say that God is going to do the work and then neglect seeking the Lord and tending to those things that we know He wants us to do. On the other extreme, we must never allow pride into our hearts, whereby we believe that the work that is done in us is because of our own efforts or merit. Both of these extremes are error.

The first error of saying that it is all on God and we have no responsibility is simply unbiblical. Throughout Scripture, we are exhorted to seek Him (1 Chr. 16:10-11; Mt. 6:33). As we have said before, there are many scriptures where we are exhorted to humble ourselves (Jam. 4:6-10, 1 Pet. 5:6). This we do by the grace of God, but the choice for us to obey this call of God is a choice that God has graciously offered to us.

This thought of responsibility that the Lord requires on our part is seen throughout this world that He has created. If we are sick, we know that whether we become well or not is ultimately up to God, since He holds all things in His hands. And yet we use the wisdom that He has given us to care for ourselves and others. We put a bandage on a cut, so that it heals. When we see a house on fire, we do not just let it burn and say, "Let the will of the Lord be done." Rather, we do what we can to put out the fire.

There are some who will not take any medicine or see any doctors, because they believe that healing should only come through faith, and so they simply pray and trust God for the healing. Certainly, in every situation, we want to pray and trust for God to work. However, when my hand is in the fire, I pull it out to keep it from being burned. When I cut my hand, I bandage it so it does not keep bleeding. When someone steps in front of my car, I put on the brake so as not to hit that person.

Yes, we walk a walk of faith. We begin by faith and continue by faith. But this faith is not in such a way as to abrogate wisdom and responsibility. God gives wisdom to many people in many different areas, and we would do well not to reject that which He has given (cf. Is. 28:25-29; Ex. 31:2-6, 36:2; Job 35:11; Dan. 1:17). Certainly, we are never to rely exclusively on wisdom. Noah never would have built the Ark if he had not believed the Lord and acted in faith. Yet neither did he sit idly by and watch as the boards of the Ark just assembled themselves by faith. The two must be balanced.

The second error is to be puffed up in pride and look at our salvation or sanctification as something that we can earn. Now, most Christians would never believe that they earn their salvation, at least not in the beginning. And yet the mindset can be that while I may not have earned my salvation at the beginning, yet I earn the right to stay saved by fulfilling many different rules. This, too, is an error. We must realize that we are totally dependent on Christ, not just for our initial salvation, but throughout our Christian life in order to do any true good.

Paul addressed this kind of error in his epistle to the Galatians. The Christians there had begun well. They had received the gospel message, but had begun to turn back to the Old Testament law, in particular circumcision, in order to be perfect. Paul asks them these questions, *"Did you receive the Spirit by works of the law or by hearing with faith? Are you so foolish? Having begun by the Spirit, are you now being perfected by the flesh?"* (Gal. 3:2b-3 ESV).

These were Christians who had been saved by the preaching of the pure Gospel. However, after their initial conversion, they were then turning back to Old Testament rituals in order to become perfect. Most of the book of Galatians is written directly against this kind of mindset. Once we have been saved by faith in Christ, it does no good to turn to outward rituals and works to become perfect.

Paul further writes: *"Look: I, Paul, say to you that if you accept circumcision, Christ will be of no advantage to you. I testify again to every man who accepts circumcision that he is obligated to keep the whole law. You are severed from Christ, you who would be justified by the law; you have fallen away from grace."* (Gal. 5:2-4 ESV).

If we are to be justified by keeping the law, then we are obligated to keep all of it, not just part of it. This would entail its thousands of commandments, dietary restrictions, washings, etc. Peter called these commandments: *"a yoke on the neck of the disciples that neither our fathers nor we have been able to bear"* (Acts 15:10). Paul tells us *"if a law had been given that could give life, then righteousness would indeed be by the law"* (Gal. 3:21). However, it is not possible. Rather, the law served as a guardian or schoolmaster to bring us to Christ (Gal. 3:24-25). Following the law was never to be an end, but to bring us to faith in Christ.

Now, the practice of following dietary laws and Old Testament circumcision in order to try to become holy is not as common today (although it does exist in some circles). However, we do find many man-made laws such as, do not touch this, and do not wear that. Many sects of Christianity prescribe certain rites that must be followed in order to attain perfection. The focus is put on outward observance. If you are wearing the correct clothing, they say that you are unspotted from the world. The problem with all this focus is that it is entirely on the external and in reality, never touches the real issues – those of the heart.

One question that I have for those who wish to impose man made rules: do you think that those rules that you are imposing should be now held in higher regard than the Old Testament laws that are a part of the Eternal Word of God? Paul tells us that those laws could not give righteousness, and following them will not make us perfect. How much less effective will man-made edicts be at perfecting the saints?

I am not saying this to encourage loose-living – by no means! What I want to point out is that holiness will never come because someone else has dictated that we should behave a certain way. There can be very valid reasons for rules, and there are settings when they can be quite appropriate. We must be very careful, however, not to believe that simply following rules will lead to holiness.

In today's society, it certainly is incumbent upon us to be careful. The Bible tells us that we should dress modestly (1 Tim. 2:9). Also, it does not do a Christian very much good if he is watching many of the movies that are prominent today. Jesus clearly speaks against the sin of lust (Mt. 5:27-28), and there are many movies today that seek to stir exactly that within the heart. Therefore, what should the Christian do? You will never escape all the pollutions of the world around you, yet you do have a choice as to which additional battles you will willingly afflict yourself.

Now, because of the problems with many movies, some churches will ban them or TV altogether. Congregants will follow those rules. Then when a new medium such as the internet comes out, there might not be a church rule against that, so they might watch much worse things on YouTube or other places than would have been in the movies. The issue is that if people follow rules, only because they are rules, and not because of their own relationship with Christ, their heart is left unchanged. When circumstances present themselves, they will engage in behavior that could be just as bad or worse.

I do not question any of the motives of those who institute many rules on the Christian. Most of them genuinely believe they are to serve a good purpose. However, as just noted above, they generally lead to contradictions, whereby people will not do a particular thing, but instead do something else that will be just as bad. This, however, is not the most problematic result. A greater problem with legalism and a focus on rules for the Christian life is that it leads to pride and strife.

This was certainly a problem with the Galatians—so much so that Paul tells them, *"But if ye bite and devour one another, take heed that ye be not consumed one of another"* (Gal. 5:15 ESV). The Pharisees in Jesus' day were also extremely legalistic. They believed that they were righteous. They tithed right down to the smallest amount, but omitted the most important things (Mt. 23:23). Outwardly, they did all the right things. They prayed long prayers and gave lots of money, but it was all so that they would be honored by men (Mt. 23:5). Jesus said that they cleaned the outside of the cup, but left the inside completely filthy (Mt. 23:25).

Legalism greatly tempts those who follow its rules to puff themselves up, because they have done such a good job at being obedient. It also leads to condemning others who have not lived up to the man-made standards that have been imposed. Further, it leads those who fail to follow the man-made laws to feel condemnation for things that might be perfectly acceptable before God. Then they may give up hope. In conflating man-made rules with God's moral commandments, they feel that they will never measure up and cease to seek to obey the Lord in any area of their life.

When the focus is on the outward, nothing good is truly done, for the heart cannot be changed just through man's effort. It is like when a building develops a crack in the foundation. You can just put some plaster over the crack, and it will look better, initially. Over time, however, the crack will only get worse. If the root cause is not fixed, the crack will only appear again and the whole building could be at risk. Christ is working in us to deal with the root causes. This will never happen as we follow rules that are laid down by others, whereby we compare ourselves with them and they with us. Rather, we are changed as we walk in the Spirit. We are changed as we yield to what the Lord is speaking to us through His Word and His still small voice. It is in yielding to Him that we are changed.

In fact, this is exactly what we see in Galatians 5. He tells us that if we walk in the Spirit, we will not satisfy the desires of the flesh (vs. 16). Instead, the Spirit produces in us fruit—specifically, *"love, joy, peace, patience, kindness, goodness, faithfulness, gentleness, self-control;"* (vs. 22b-23). Just like an apple tree produces apples, so too, the Holy Spirit produces Holy Spirit fruit in the life of the believer. Also in verses 25 and 26 Paul says, *"And those who belong to Christ Jesus have crucified the flesh with its passions and desires. If we live by the Spirit, let us also keep in step with the Spirit."*

So, how does this work out practically? I believe that a Biblical example can help here. Consider the story of Peter in Acts chapter 10. Here, a God-fearing Gentile, Cornelius, was given a vision of an angel and told to send for Peter who was in another city. The next day, when the messengers were approaching the city, Peter was on the housetop praying and the Lord gave him the same vision three times. In this vision, Peter was shown a sheet coming down, and on it were all kinds of animals. He was commanded to kill and eat, and responded that he would not, because he had never eaten anything common or unclean. To this, the Lord replied in the vision, *"What God has made clean, do not call common"* (v. 15b).

This vision served an important purpose. Remember that Jewish Old Testament laws forbade them from eating many different things. Peter was very observant in these things. He wanted to be careful to follow those rules. In the vision, given three times, Peter told the Lord that he would not break those rules. However, immediately after this vision, Cornelius' messengers came to the gate and were asking for Peter. While Peter was thinking on the vision he had just received, the Spirit said to him: *"Rise and go down and accompany them without hesitation, for I have sent them"* (v. 20 ESV).

Peter did indeed go with the men to Cornelius' house. There, he preached the Gospel and while he was still speaking, many of the people gathered were filled with the Holy Spirit. Peter, seeing that the Holy Spirit had come upon them, said, *"Can anyone withhold water for baptizing these people, who have received the Holy Spirit just as we have?"* (v. 47 ESV). Peter obeyed the command of God to go with these men and in so doing, many Gentiles were saved.

While Peter's going and preaching to Gentiles might not seem like a big thing to us, remember the context this was in. In fact, in the very next chapter, Peter took some serious grief from fellow believers for doing such a thing. To go into the house of Gentiles and eat with them would have caused Peter to be defiled. He would have been ceremonially unclean. It was something that would have been looked down upon and he would have been forbidden from entering the temple or participating in public worship. However, when Peter explained the situation to them, and how God had prepared him beforehand, they fell silent and *"...they glorified God, saying, 'Then to the Gentiles also God has granted repentance that leads to life'"* (Acts 11:18b ESV).

In looking at this story, there are a couple of things that are relevant to our topic of the walk in the Spirit here. It provides a good example where we can contrast an outward appearance of righteousness with that which is pleasing in God's eyes. Suppose that Peter had not gone with the messengers. Suppose that he had disobeyed God's command in the vision. To everyone else around him, he would have appeared to be very righteous. He would have been following a strict adherence to the law. He had legitimate reasons for not going with the messengers and that is why God gave him a vision three times.

However, in God's eyes, he would not have been righteous. He was disobeying a direct command of the Lord to go and witness to these people. God wanted to do something new, in opening the Gospel to the Gentiles, and He wanted to use Peter to do it. If Peter had disobeyed, he would have been hindering the great work that God was about to do in the earth. Thus, we see that from the outside it would have been absolutely impossible to look at Peter and to assess his state before God. No one else knew what God had specifically told Peter, and so no one would have known whether he was following the Lord.

In fact, as we saw, initially others looked down on Peter when he obeyed the Lord. The risk he took in following the Lord's leading was great, and yet he was faithful to do it. This is the walk in the Spirit. It is not a walk that is prescribed by rules, but by love and obedience. It is the walk that was shown in glimpses in the Old Testament such as in Micah 6:6-8, but is now made evident in the Gospel. Our walk is a walk of faith. It is not a walk whereby we check off the list of good things we did today. Rather, it is a life of waiting on the Lord and diligently following Him as His grace allows. We may not be perfect in our walk, but by His grace God is still working on us.

What does this mean? It means that I cannot judge another Christian by my own standards. God sees each heart and each circumstance. Certainly, there are some things that are non-negotiable. There are God's moral standards that can never be violated. If someone is breaking these laws, we know clearly that that is wrong. The Bible is unequivocal about these, which we will discuss later. What is also clear, though, is that there are many things in the Christian life that are less clear. How long should we pray? How often should we fast? How much of the Word of God should we read each day?

If I have a lot of free time and read 10 chapters of the Bible every day and spend an hour in prayer that is good. However, there may be a woman who is in a difficult situation, works two jobs, has a family that is dependent on her and struggles to pray and read more than ten minutes a day. God may meet more with that woman in those ten minutes than He does with me in the hour. Her time in prayer may be more precious in His sight than mine.

Consider the widow who gave only two low-value coins (Mk. 12:41-44). She put only a very small amount of money into the offering box, and yet Jesus said that she put in more than anyone else. This is because she gave out of her poverty. What little she had, she brought to the Lord. God knows each circumstance, and we do not. We cannot compare ourselves with others or try to impose our own regimens on them.

Furthermore, we must be careful not to judge our own Christian walk by an unreasonable standard. Obviously, reading the Bible is good; praying is good. These are things that God uses to change us. However, we have to be careful not to drift into a rules-based relationship with God.

Consider the following line of reasoning. If it is good to pray for ten minutes, then it is better to pray for an hour. If it is good to pray for an hour then it is better to pray for two hours. If it is good to read a chapter of the Bible, then it is better to read two. If it is good to read two chapters, then it is better to read ten. Now, while we can agree with this, in general, I think we can all see the problem with this. It never ends. You will always be able to do more. If you judge yourself by how much you are praying or reading the Bible, invariably you will not measure up to where you want to be and you will condemn yourself, because you can always do more.

What does the Lord want of you? He wants a true living relationship. Does that involve prayer? Absolutely. Does it involve Scripture reading?

Certainly. However, we can put unrealistic burdens upon ourselves to which we will never measure up and believe that our sanctification is founded in that. It is not. It never will be. Our sanctification is firmly grounded on the finished work of Christ and then it is worked out in us as we walk in the Spirit. This means yielding to Him. We pray. We read the Bible. But, we do not do it so that we can check off a box to say that I read my required amount for the day. Rather, we read so that we might know the Living Word. We pray so that we might know the love of the Lovely One. Our Christian walk is a vibrant walk, because the God we serve is alive.

There is nothing wrong with structure in our devotions. We certainly do not want to go to the extreme of saying, "The Spirit hasn't moved me to read my Bible recently, so I haven't read it!" There is wisdom in doing what we know to do and then yielding to God at His prompting. Our sanctification is not based on rules that either we or another has made. Rather, it is on being found in Him (Php. 3:9).

Do I wish that I spent more time in prayer? Yes. Do I wish that I read the Word more? Yes. Indeed, there are times when we feel the stirring of the Spirit and those are times that we need to respond, more than ever. We want to be better Christians. We want to be better servants of our Lord. But, we must be careful not to run into the trap of judging ourselves or others by a standard that is not the same as the Lord's. We must be careful not to try to earn our sanctification by striving with works, however good they may be. True holiness comes only from being joined to the One who is truly holy.

---

[19] Olsen, Roger. (2006). *Arminian Theology: Myths and Realities*, IVP Academic. Page 211.

[20] Lewis, C.S. (1943). *Mere Christianity*. Macmillan. Pages 173-174.

ASSURANCE

In the prior chapter, we saw how our salvation is not a static experience, but rather a journey by faith, where the Lord changes us for our good and His glory. As we are on this journey, we should have the strong Biblical assurance that we are saved and are a part of His family. If you are waiting for sinless perfection before you have assurance of your salvation, you will never have it. That is not Biblical assurance. Likewise, if you have been saved and believe that your ticket to eternity has been punched, regardless of what you do in the future, that is not Biblical assurance.

Scripture shows us the balance between these two extremes, as it clearly teaches two things:

1. Christians are not perfect and do sin.

2. Christians should not be deceived into thinking that willful sinning will be excused by God.

Let us be clear on that first point. When a person is saved, he is not instantly transformed to the point that he never sins again. Yes, there is absolutely a transformation, but it is not instantly complete. There is a work done on the inside, whereby the person is instantly translated from the kingdom of darkness into the kingdom of Christ (Col. 1:13). The Holy Spirit dwells within and he is adopted into God's family (Rom. 8:14-17). The good work was begun by the Lord, and He will bring it to completion (Php. 1:6).

As long as we are in this body, we should continue to *"…grow in the grace and knowledge of our Lord and Savior Jesus Christ."* (2 Pet. 3:18a ESV). The Apostle Paul, himself, wrote that he was not yet perfect, but that he was pressing on (Php. 3:12). Obviously, Paul was saved. He was a wonderful man of God, and yet not perfect. As we noted in prior chapters, our Christian life is a journey. Some things are done instantly, but the rest continue throughout our lives.

If it were necessary for a person to be perfectly free from sin before he could be a true Christian, then I am not sure if I have ever yet met a Christian. We are forgiven in Christ, and the Holy Spirit, that dwells within us, is working through us to perform the works that He has foreordained (Eph. 2:10). If we stumble along the way, this does not mean that we have lost our salvation. Rather, Christians are not perfect and the blood of Christ covers our sins.

John's first epistle has quite a bit to say about these concepts, both giving comfort to Christians who are struggling and refuting the idea that willful sin will be overlooked by God. We find comfort in the first few verses of chapter 2: *"My little children, I am writing these things to you so that you may not sin. But if anyone does sin, we have an advocate with the Father, Jesus Christ the righteous. He is the propitiation for our sins, and not for ours only but also for the sins of the whole world"* (1 Jn. 2:1-2 ESV).

Note how believers are encouraged not to sin. John says that this was a primary objective of his when writing this epistle. However, he is also clear to point out that if we do sin, we have an advocate with the Father, Jesus Christ the righteous. Clearly, John is writing to Christians so that they will abstain from sin, but he is also telling these same Christians that if they do sin, Christ is the propitiation for their sins. Christ is specifically the sacrifice for our sins and for the sins of the whole world. John does not want his converts to sin, but also assures them that if they do, Christ's blood covers their sin.

Earlier in his epistle, John appeals to Christians to walk in the light (1 Jn. 1:7-10). In so doing, the blood of Christ will cleanse them from all sin. What then does John mean when he says "walk in the light?" We will explore this in greater detail later, but for now, I think it is helpful to point out what it does <u>not</u> mean. First, it is clear that it does not mean sinless perfection. If that were the case, then why does John immediately follow that statement by saying that the blood of Christ cleanses from all sin?

If the Christian were already walking in a completely sinless manner then why would the continual cleansing of the blood still be necessary? Indeed, John exhorts us not to deceive ourselves by thinking that we are sinless. Rather, we are faulty. We sin, but when we do, we confess those sins to the Lord and we are thoroughly cleansed and made completely whole. We maintain our fellowship with God and one another.

So, the question readily arises, "If the blood of Christ forgives the Christian's sin, then does sin really matter for the Christian?" Or, to put it another way, "If after I am saved and forgiven, why should I not just keep on sinning so that God can be shown to be even more merciful?" Paul answers these kinds of questions at least two times in Romans. In chapter 3, Paul says that even if the wickedness of some people proves how righteous and just God is, it does not excuse those people of their sin (3:5-8). To those who say things like, "Well, my sin makes God appear even more righteous, so let us do evil that good may come," Paul replies that their damnation is just.

Also, the passage from Romans 5:20-6:2 restates these same thoughts: *"Now the law came in to increase the trespass, but where sin increased, grace abounded all the more, so that, as sin reigned in death, grace also might reign through righteousness leading to eternal life through Jesus Christ our Lord. What shall we say then? Are we to continue in sin that grace may abound? By no means! How can we who died to sin still live in it?"* (ESV).

A Christian simply cannot remain the same. If we are saved by grace, then we are dead to sin, that we might live to God. Therefore, a Christian cannot continue to live the same life that he did before he was saved. Instead, Paul makes it clear that the grace of God is <u>not</u> an excuse for continuing in sin. We find forgiveness in Christ, but not license to sin. The Christian walk is a walk of grace, whereby we are dead to the world and its ways, and the world is dead to us (Gal. 6:14).

As we said earlier, the Apostle John wrote about this extensively, *"When we obey God, we are sure that we know him. But if we claim to know him and don't obey him, we are lying and the truth isn't in our hearts"* (1 Jn. 2:4-5 ESV). Verses such as this are throughout his first epistle. John consistently relates the thought that if we love God or are in the light, it will be reflected in outward actions (2:9-11; 3:6-10; 3:14-15; 3:16-17; 3:23-24; 4:7-8; 4:20-21). We will synthesize these later with what we said about Christians not being perfect, but what they clearly show us is that the Christian walk is absolutely not to be one where we claim to be forgiven, but behave exactly as we did before we were saved. The fact that we are saved and know God will be displayed through our outward actions. Otherwise, we are deceiving ourselves.

Paul also makes this very clear. He echoes the same in his epistle to Titus: *"They profess to know God, but they deny him by their works. They are detestable, disobedient, unfit for any good work"* (1:16 ESV). Here, Paul links the profession of knowing God with works. He does this in the sense that it is expected that if we know God it will be confirmed by the things that we do. If we are living a disobedient life, then our mouth may confess that we know God, but we will be denying it by our works.

In 1 Corinthians 6, he writes, *"Or do you not know that the unrighteous will not inherit the kingdom of God? Do not be deceived: neither the sexually immoral, nor idolaters, nor adulterers, nor men who practice homosexuality, nor thieves, nor the greedy, nor drunkards, nor revilers, nor swindlers will inherit the kingdom of God. And such were some of you. But you were washed, you were sanctified, you were justified in the name of the Lord Jesus Christ and by the Spirit of our God"* (vs. 9-11 ESV).

Paul specifically tells his readers not to be deceived. Of course, the implication is that they will be tempted, either through the influence of their own hearts, or directly from others, to believe that they could partake in such things and still inherit the kingdom of God. Paul fully denies it. Also, he states that some of them were exactly these things, but now they are not. Now, they are washed, sanctified and justified in the name of the Lord and by the Spirit. They were such in the past, but now are clean.

However, they cannot return to the old ways if they want to inherit the kingdom of God.

Paul gives a very similar message in Galatians 5: *"Now the works of the flesh are evident: sexual immorality, impurity, sensuality, idolatry, sorcery, enmity, strife, jealousy, fits of anger, rivalries, dissensions, divisions, envy, drunkenness, orgies, and things like these. I warn you, as I warned you before, that those who do such things will not inherit the kingdom of God"* (vs. 19-21 ESV).

The message is very clear. If we practice sins such as the above, we will not inherit the kingdom of God. Now, this passage immediately precedes a very well-known passage, where Paul lists the fruit of the Spirit (vs. 22-23). Many of us probably have learned songs as children about the fruit of the spirit and we picture grapes, apples, etc. All of that is well and good, but I think it is easy to miss the main point of this illustration when we have heard it so many times. The main point of this passage is that it is the Spirit that produces in us certain kinds of fruit, or works.

In verses 19-21, we see that the works of the flesh are really bad. They are all kinds of sinful deeds, and these are what we do by nature. Every one of us is capable and inclined to all of these, to one degree or another. However, when the Spirit of God comes in, He produces fruit in our lives. What is this fruit? It is: *"love, joy, peace, patience, kindness, goodness, faithfulness, gentleness, self-control"* (vs. 22b-23a ESV).

Just like an apple tree produces apples and an orange tree produces oranges, so the Spirit of God in the life of a believer produces love, joy, peace, etc. Jesus told us that we will recognize a false prophet by their fruits (Mt. 7:15-20). If all that our lives are producing is thorns and every evil work, then the evidence that the Holy Spirit is inside us and working is missing.

In the above passages, Paul rebukes the thought that a Christian can simply claim to believe in Christ and then live a life of immorality and still expect to be saved. Rather, he tells us: *"But I say, walk by the Spirit, and you will not gratify the desires of the flesh. For the desires of the flesh are against the Spirit, and the desires of the Spirit are against the flesh, for these are opposed to each other, to keep you from doing the things you want to do"* (Gal. 5:16-17 ESV). If we are walking in the Spirit, we will not be sinning. The Holy Spirit will not lead us into sin. Contrariwise, if we are walking according to the flesh, we are not walking in the Spirit. They are completely opposed to each other, and our life will bear fruit according to whether we are walking with God or in our own ways.

Bear in mind that the above passages were written by the Apostle Paul, and the last one came specifically from the Book of Galatians. Paul is often called the "Apostle of Grace." This is because of how much he spoke of the grace of God and showed how we are not saved by works, especially in the Book of Galatians. But we must not interpret his message to mean that we can be saved and still continue in any evil deed that we may be inclined to do. This is not the kind of grace that Paul ever espoused. It is simply an unbiblical view of grace.

What shall we say then with these things? On one hand, we have placed a stake in the ground that we are saved by grace through faith. It is totally separate from works. Also, we have clearly seen that Christians are not instantly perfect upon salvation. We are still continually washed by the blood and in need of forgiveness and cleansing after salvation. This is a guidepost that must remain.

On the other hand, we have also seen that Scripture is very clear that we cannot remain the same. Both John and Paul (not to mention Peter and James) show us that we cannot simply say that we know God and yet continue in sin. If our lives do not show the fruit of the Spirit, they are denying that we are saved. Paul is unequivocal: a person living in immorality will not inherit the kingdom of God. This is also a firm guidepost that we cannot cross. It is a boundary that is established throughout Scripture – the unrighteous will not inherit the kingdom of God.

Therefore, what we can say is that, as Christians, we will fail. We will sin, and when we do, there is an advocate for us, Jesus Christ the righteous. However, what is also clear is that if we cast off restraint and choose willfully to walk in disobedience, then our works are denying the confession that we are making with our mouths. Hebrews says this: *"For if we go on sinning deliberately after receiving the knowledge of the truth, there no longer remains a sacrifice for sins, but a fearful expectation of judgment, and a fury of fire that will consume the adversaries"* (10:26-27 ESV). Peter tells us, *"For if, after they have escaped the defilements of the world through the knowledge of our Lord and Savior Jesus Christ, they are again entangled in them and overcome, the last state has become worse for them than the first"* (2 Pet. 2:20 ESV).

We should not expect to be perfect. Further, just because we are not perfect is not a cause for us to doubt our salvation. No, we are saved by the grace and mercy of God through Christ. We should have assurance that we are saved. The Holy Spirit within us should bear witness to the fact that we are the children of God (Rom. 8:15-17). As we already saw, John's first epistle speaks of "knowing" many times. It is a major theme that we are to know that we are *"of the truth"* or *"in Him"* and *"have passed from death to life"* (2:5, 3:19, 3:14). We should be assured that we are His and He is ours. When we are in this Christian life, we should not be living in a state of doubt of our salvation. We should have the inner witness of the Spirit and we should have outward fruit bearing witness that we are children of God. It might not be perfect fruit, because He is not done with us yet, but nonetheless there is fruit. This is often how John said that we should know that we are His.

Assurance is an important part of our Christian walk, and yet one thing is also clear: Scripture does not offer assurance to those who do not care to keep His commandments, or hate their neighbors. Rather, *"Everyone who hates his brother is a murderer, and you know that no murderer has eternal life abiding in him"* (1 Jn. 3:15). In many ways, we looked at this issue in the prior chapter on repentance. We do not have to be perfect, because there is a sacrifice for us: Jesus Christ, the righteous. But, when we have sinned, we take it to the Lord and receive complete and total cleansing. If, instead of going to the Lord with our problems, we ignore Him and His word and choose to go our own way, harboring anger, lust and deceit, we will not have assurance of salvation. How we respond to how He deals with us matters. Assurance is meant to be with us as Christians as we walk with the Lord, even if imperfectly, but it is a false assurance that says that we can willfully sin and still expect to be received by the Lord.

There are those who believe that once you have been saved, it is impossible to ever lose your salvation. They believe that you are eternally secure in Christ. Generally, they would say that this gives the most assurance to Christians, because if something is eternally secure, then it is most to be trusted. I actually believe that this doctrine destroys true Christian assurance, which we will now examine.

First, we have to deal with this concept of eternal security from two different camps. The first is a more modern view of it, which basically says, "Once you have accepted Christ, you are saved and no matter what sin you commit, you will always be saved." The proponents of this, especially in hyper-grace movements, say that sin is unimportant. They emphasize the love of God. They say that Christians are not under the law, which they take to mean that we can live as we please and that no matter what we do, we will be accepted by God. This view is simply unbiblical. We have seen before in this chapter how the New Testament writers all make it very clear that, no matter who tries to deceive you, God will not accept those who work lawlessness (cf. Mt. 7:23).

There is another group that does take a more biblical approach in how they view sin and holiness. They see the many passages in Scripture that speak of the unrighteous not inheriting the kingdom of heaven. They acknowledge that there has to be some kind of change in the life of the believer. However, rather than believe that a person may lose their salvation, they believe that if a person leaves the faith, they were never actually a true believer. Instead, they say that it is a sign that they simply had a false faith, but never were truly converted to begin with.

I have respect for this second group, because at least it acknowledges the many passages of Scripture that clearly show that our Christian life is meant to be a transformative one. However, I do believe that this view is still yet unbiblical and that it destroys Christian assurance. You may say, "If it purports to give eternal security, how can it destroy assurance?" I believe it is so, because under such a system, it is impossible to know if you were ever saved, as you do not know what you will do in the future.

Under such a system, if a person were to apostatize at the end of his life and deny Christ, it is not just that at that time he has lost His communion with the Lord. Instead, it would be assumed that this person had never been a real Christian. He had never truly surrendered his life to Christ, and was never truly saved. Thus, in the end, he only revealed what had always been true. Such a system totally destroys all Christian assurance.

I am sure that all of us have known people that once walked with the Lord and do so no longer. Some have totally gone to the point of openly denying Him. However, at one time, they had faithfully served Him, had committed their lives to Him and in every way that we could possibly know, were walking with Him. Importantly, they too were sure that they were saved. If I know one thing, I know that I am as capable of sinning greatly and turning from the Lord as the next man. It is only the mercy and grace of God that keeps me. If I acknowledge my weakness, I acknowledge that I too could fall into sin, and leave the Lord who bought me. However, if such a thing were to happen, and eternal security were true, then it would have to be concluded that I had never been saved. Everything that I had lived up to that point would have been a lie, because I would have believed that I was saved, when in fact, I had only received evanescent grace.

Likewise, those whom we have known that have departed from our Lord, were they ever really His or did they only appear to be Christians? We have a pertinent Biblical example that should help us here in 1 Corinthians 6. Now, we already looked at a couple of verses in this passage earlier, but if we continue on in the chapter, it will be useful for answering some of these questions.

Paul opens the chapter by rebuking believers who were in disputes and suing each other before unbelievers (vs. 1-8). Then we have the passage that we examined before, where Paul warns them not to be deceived into thinking that the unrighteous will inherit the kingdom of God. He lists examples of many that will not be saved, but states that some of the Corinthians were in these categories, but have now been washed and justified *"in the name of the Lord Jesus Christ and by the Spirit of our God"* (vs. 9-11 ESV). Then we have in verses 12-20 the main part that I want to examine now. We will not be looking at each point, but just at the big picture.

This section begins by discussing eating food and the liberty a Christian has in what he eats (v. 12). He states that our liberty should be tempered so as to not allow food to dominate our lives. *"Food is meant for the stomach and the stomach for food"* and both will be destroyed (v. 13a). This, he particularly contrasts with sexual immorality, where he states, *"The body is not meant for sexual immorality, but for the Lord, and the Lord for the body"* (v. 13b). Further, *"And God raised the Lord and will also raise us up by his power"* (1 Cor. 6:14 ESV).

The body is made to eat and the Lord has provided food for that purpose. Food is necessary as long as we are here on earth, but it will not last forever. God has ordained both that food is to be digested and broken down by our bodies and also a time when our bodies will be destroyed. However, we were not created for sexual immorality. John Gill's commentary puts it this way: *"Though meats are appointed for the belly, and the belly for them, and this and the other sort of meats are of an indifferent kind, which may or may not be used; yet this cannot be said of fornication, which the Corinthians, and other Gentiles, took to be equally indifferent as meats."*[21] There is a difference between the fleshly appetites.

The next verses then proceed to warn us specifically against sexual immorality (vs. 15-20). The line of reasoning that Paul uses here is very revealing. He notes that as Christians, our bodies are members of Christ. Should we then take the parts of Christ's body and make them parts of a prostitute's body? Paul absolutely rebukes that, and reminds us, *"Or do you not know that he who is joined to a prostitute becomes one body with her?"* (v. 16a ESV). Also, *"But he who is joined to the Lord becomes one spirit with him"* (v. 17 ESV). Finally, Paul closes with this, *"Flee from sexual immorality. Every other sin a person commits is outside the body, but the sexually immoral person sins against his own body. Or do you not know that your body is a temple of the Holy Spirit within you, whom you have from God? You are not your own, for you were bought with a price. So glorify God in your body"* (vs. 18-20 ESV).

When Paul is warning against sexual immorality, he is specifically warning Christians. His warning is not to the unsaved. His warning is not saying that if you participate in the prostitution that was common place in the temples of that time that you were never saved in the first place. Rather, he is specifically warning the Corinthian Christians that inasmuch as they are joined to Christ and are the temple of the Holy Spirit, to defile that temple is a great sin. Remember, just before this, he had told them *"Do not be deceived: neither the sexually immoral, nor idolaters, nor adulterers, nor men who practice homosexuality… will inherit the kingdom of God."* (vs. 9a, 10c ESV).

This warning is not to those who have never been saved. The unsaved are not joined to Christ. Their body is not the temple of the Holy Spirit, but the believer's is. To those who defile the temple of God, Paul writes this: *"Do you not know that you are God's temple and that God's Spirit dwells in you? If anyone destroys God's temple, God will destroy him. For God's temple is holy, and you are that temple"* (1 Cor. 3:16-17 ESV). These warnings are clearly to those who have been saved – they should not destroy the temple of God. Sexual sins are particularly singled out by Paul as sins against the body. The Christian must *"flee youthful passions"* (2 Tim. 2:22).

What if the Christian does not? What if someone confesses Christ, is walking with Him, and then leaves the path and falls into all kinds of sin? While we do not always know the state of a person's heart, what is clear from Scripture is that a person who has turned from God into sin and is openly practicing it will not be saved. This does not mean there is no hope for this person. There is certainly hope in Christ, but there must be repentance and an acknowledgment of the sin. This hope we will explore more later on, but for now, let us continue with examining those who fall into sin.

I believe the Bible is clear that there are different groups. Certainly, there are those who associate with Christians but are, themselves, never saved. They appear in many ways to be Christians, but they have never surrendered their heart to the Lord and were never saved. These would be false converts and are like the tares that Jesus spoke of in His parable of the wheat and the tares (Mt. 13:24-30). This would also likely be the group to which John refers in 1 John 2:19.

There are also those who we have been discussing above that have been saved, but for whatever reason, turn from the truth. They have been saved. They have been washed, and yet they walk with the Lord no more. As Peter says, *"What the true proverb says has happened to them: 'The dog returns to its own vomit, and the sow, after washing herself, returns to wallow in the mire.'"* (2 Pet. 2:22). The pig has been washed, but returns to wallow in the filth. Also, *"For if, after they have escaped the defilements of the world through the knowledge of our Lord and Savior Jesus Christ, they are again entangled in them and overcome, the last state has become worse for them than the first"* (2 Pet. 2:20 ESV). This is not a group that is unsaved, for they *"escaped the defilements of the world"* and now *"are again entangled in them and overcome"*. These are those who had become the temple of the Holy Spirit, but defiled it and left Christ.

One may ask, "If I can be truly saved and yet lose my salvation, does that not destroy my assurance?" That is a valid question, but I do not believe that it does. For one, you certainly have more assurance than you can under a system in which you will never know until the end whether you have ever been saved to begin with.[22] Furthermore, and most importantly, we must remember that we are *"kept by the power of God"* (1 Pet. 1:5). It is the Lord who is mercifully guiding and keeping us. We need not fear that He is looking to cast us aside. By no means! Rather, it is Christ that died for us.

As Romans 8:32 says, *"He who did not spare his own Son but gave him up for us all, how will he not also with him graciously give us all things?"* (ESV). Remember, that God is more interested in our salvation than we are – He is the one who designed and executed the plan of salvation. If He sent

His Son to die for us, does it make sense that He would be looking for a reason to disqualify us? Certainly not! God is not looking down from heaven, seeking to find fault, especially not with His children. He gave us His Son, what more does He need to do to prove that He desires us to be saved?

God is looking down in love and is providing us all things that are necessary that we might *be conformed to the image of his Son*" (Rom. 8:29b ESV). God is not looking to disqualify us, but rather to transform us into the sons and daughters that He has called us to be. That is going to be a lot of work, but to Him, it is worth it! The true Gospel emphasizes both the holiness and the love of God. In Jesus Christ, *"mercy and truth are met together"* (Ps. 85:10a).

What is also clear is that we should always be relying upon God for our salvation every day. Not in the sense that we are living in a constant state of fear, but in the sense that our only trust is in Him and in His present grace. We are not trusting in a past experience, but in a continuous, ever-present Lord who is walking daily with us, to uphold and comfort us along life's difficult path. This is where we come to having a proper fear of the Lord.

This fear of the Lord is not a crippling fear, but rather it is a respect and a humble acknowledgement that our lives are in God's hands. We are totally dependent on Him. The Old Testament many times talks about the fear of the Lord and always in a positive light. It often states how important it is and how it is *"the beginning of wisdom"* (Pro. 9:10b). Yet the New Testament also encourages the fear of the Lord in numerous passages. To list only a few:

> ➢ *"Wherefore we receiving a kingdom which cannot be moved, let us have grace, whereby we may serve God acceptably with reverence and godly fear:"* (Heb. 12:28).

> ➢ *"And if ye call on the Father, who without respect of persons judgeth according to every man's work, pass the time of your sojourning here in fear:"* (1 Pet. 1:17).

> ➤ *"Honour all men. Love the brotherhood. Fear God. Honour the king."* (1 Pet. 2:17).

> ➤ *"Therefore, my beloved, as you have always obeyed, so now, not only as in my presence but much more in my absence, work out your own salvation with fear and trembling, for it is God who works in you, both to will and to work for his good pleasure."* (Php. 2:12-13).

Specifically, let us consider the above passage from Philippians 2. These two verses give us an excellent picture of our Christian duty. We are encouraged to *"work out (our) own salvation"*, but then immediately told that *"it is God who works in you…"* So, one may ask the question: "Who is doing the work – is it me or God?" If it is God, then why am I encouraged to work out my salvation, and if it be I, then why does the apostle tell me that it is God who is working in me?

In reality, I believe that this is exactly what we have seen throughout this book. There are two lines of demarcation, two guideposts, that cannot be crossed, because both are true. We are responsible for our own actions. As beings created in the image of God, we are responsible for the free agency that God has given us. At the same time, the other guidepost that cannot be crossed is this: we can do absolutely no good thing without the grace and mercy of God. God is sovereign over all.

The phrase *"work out your salvation with fear and trembling"*, is immediately followed by *"for it is God who works"*. A healthy fear of the Lord is an acknowledgement that we depend on Him for everything. We serve Him. We seek to do those things that please Him, because we know that we are totally dependent upon His good grace. If it were not He working in us, we would neither do good, nor even desire to do good, for it is God who works in us *"both to will and to work"*.

We fear Him, therefore, because we literally cannot serve Him without His grace. We would not even *want* to serve Him. It is *"to the praise of his glory"*, that we, *"having no hope"* as enemies of God, should be loved and transformed by the One who is working in us to make us vessels of honor (cf. Eph. 1:12, 2:12; Rom. 5:10). As the Psalmist says, *"If you, O LORD, should mark iniquities, O Lord, who could stand? But with you there is forgiveness, that you may be feared"* (Ps. 130:3-4). If the Lord were not going to forgive, there would really be no point in fearing Him. It would be hopeless. But the fact that God is merciful to those who humbly confess their reliance on Him means that there is hope. It instills fear, in the sense that we do not want to displease the One who forgives and gives grace to all who come to Him in faith.

---

[21] Gill, John. *John Gill's Commentary.* 1 Corinthians 6:13

[22] I understand that Calivinists would disagree with this, saying along these lines "The Spirit of God bears witness with my spirit that I am truly saved. Those who turned from the Lord never had this assurance." Setting aside the fact that they really can have no idea of the actual assurance that the backslider felt, there is a deeper issue. Calvin explained many of the warning passages by suggesting that God gives evanescent grace to the reprobate, such that they even truly believe that they are saved. He wrote that "experience shows that the reprobate are sometimes affected in a way so similar to the elect, that even in their own judgment there is no difference between them" (Institutes, 3.2.11). This evanescent grace does help to answer some of the warning passages, such as John 15, but it creates a myriad of problems. Calvinists today may not cling to evanescent grace in the same way, but without it, many passages pose great difficulty. With it, assurance is destroyed and God's character is seriously impugned.

114

EPILOGUE

As we close this book, I want us to remember something that we have repeated often. Salvation was not our idea. It was God's. God did not die for us because we were worthy of it. There is no group nor individual that is worthy of the tremendous price that He paid. It is because of His great love for us. It is by His grace that we are saved. Furthermore, it is by His power that we are transformed. God is sovereign and has chosen us in Christ that we might be conformed to His image.

Salvation starts from the beginning as being God's plan to redeem us, the rebellious, who had gone away from Him. He takes the unlovely and calls them beloved. Once He has begun that process in us, He does not stop. The continual transformation that takes place in our lives is brought about by the Holy Spirit. It is a work of God from beginning to end.

Yet the Scripture also shows us that, for some reason, God has given us free will. He has given us the choice – not to truly change ourselves, for that we could never do – but the choice to yield ourselves to His work. It is in surrender that we find the life of Christ being manifest in us. Indeed, for the weary worker, remember that Christ tells us that His yoke is easy and His burden is light (Mt. 11:28-30).

If you are discouraged in your walk, remember that God desires your sanctification more than you ever will. The same God who loved you enough to die for you, loves you enough to see your transformation through. He began that work of salvation and will see it through to the end. The Spirit that raised Christ from the dead dwells in every believer. He is working to see our entire redemption fully completed, that we might be to the praise of His glory.

It is one thing to forgive a criminal his debts, but so much more than that, our God is in the business or making criminals into saints. He is transforming us. This is part of the entire plan of salvation. Every day that I am alive on this earth is another day that I get to see what the Lord will do with a wretch like me. Let us not resist His work. Rather, let us yield to His Spirit. We are not called to remain as we are, but we are called to be conformed into His image.

As we walk with the Lord, He takes our ashes and gives us His beauty. He takes our mess and makes something beautiful. We will never have anything to boast about, because the work is His. Truly, His plans are wonderful. As the Apostle Paul said, *"O the depth of the riches both of the wisdom and knowledge of God! how unsearchable are his judgments, and his ways past finding out!"* (Rom. 11:33).

This amazing plan of salvation was not designed by the Father to exclude people. Rather, it is the Lord's desire to save all. He is taking us from our filth and making us holy and pure in His sight. He has saved us. He is saving us. He will save us. He designed the plan and He executed it. This salvation is for all. It is not to condemn us, but rather it was designed that we might have eternal fellowship with the Lord. *"For God did not send his Son into the world to condemn the world, but in order that the world might be saved through him."* (Jn. 3:17 ESV). His love calls us out of darkness. As we come into the light, it is not for our glory, but for the glory of His great name. Praise be to God!